ORDINARY MEN

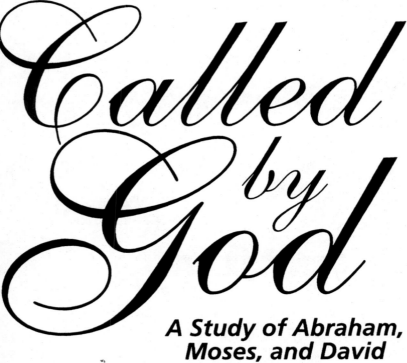

Called by God

A Study of Abraham, Moses, and David

JAMES MONTGOMERY BOICE

kregel
PUBLICATIONS

Grand Rapids, MI 49501

Ordinary Men Called by God: A Study of Abraham, Moses, and David

Copyright © 1982 by James Montgomery Boice

Published in 1998 by Kregel Publications, a division of Kregel, Inc., P.O. Box 2607, Grand Rapids, MI 49501.

Cover design: Alan G. Hartman

Library of Congress Cataloging-in-Publication Data
Boice, James Montgomery, 1938–
    Ordinary men called by God: a study of Abraham, Moses, and David / by James Montgomery Boice.
        p.   cm.
    Originally published: Wheaton, Ill.: Scripture Press Publications, 1987.
    1. Abraham (Biblical patriarch). 2. Moses (Biblical leader). 3. David, King of Israel. 4. Bible. O.T.—Bibliography. 5. Christian life—Biblical teaching. I. Title.
BS574.5.B65   1998   221.9'22—dc21   97-47515
                                                             CIP
ISBN 978-0-8254-2075-7

Printed in the United States of America

5 6 7 8 / 11 10 09

To the Author and Finisher of our faith,
who, for the joy that was set before Him,
endured the cross, despising the shame,
and is set down at the right hand
of the throne of God.

CONTENTS

THE AUTHOR

James Montgomery Boice is the pastor of the historic Tenth Presbyterian Church, Philadelphia, and speaker on the Bible Study Hour radio program heard weekly coast to coast.

Dr. Boice, who was born in Pittsburgh on July 7, 1938, received the A.B. degree from Harvard with high honors in English literature. In 1963 he graduated from Princeton Theological Seminary, after which he and his wife, Linda Ann, went to Basel, Switzerland, where he studied further.

Dr. Boice served as assistant editor for *Christianity Today* before becoming pastor of Tenth Presbyterian Church.

INTRODUCTION

Like all preachers, the Lord Jesus Christ had His favorite sermons. We know, because He repeated His words on occasion. The text which is most repeated is found in various forms in Matthew 18:4 and 23:12 and in Luke 14:11 and 18:14. It is a formula for greatness: "Whosoever shall exalt himself shall be abased; and he that shall humble himself shall be exalted." It is according to this text that Abraham, Moses, and David are to be considered great men—the three greatest men of the Old Testament.

Abraham, Moses, and David were great in other ways also. Each showed great courage in battle. Each was a leader of men. Each was faithful in his responsibilities over a long period of time. Yet before God each of these men was great primarily because he humbled himself. In other words, he did not fear to bow low before God that thereafter he might stand tall before men. If each reader of this book could learn this lesson and practice it, the impact upon our homes, churches, businesses, and nation would be immeasurable.

But there are yet other lessons to be learned from the lives of these great figures. Each life clearly shows evidence of the priority of God's call to both faith and service. This was God-glorifying. To recognize the sovereignty and preeminence of God in our lives today, in the 20th century, is equally essential. Each man also demonstrates the importance of human responsibility. How he behaved mattered, sometimes for good and sometimes for evil. Each was obliged to answer to God according to what he had done. Finally, each of these lives reveals the nature and cause of spiritual failures, as well as the means of overcoming failures and advancing to victory.

These studies are not intended to be comprehensive treatments of the lives of Abraham, Moses, and David. Rather, they are designed to explore the most important features of the relationship of these men to God, and to study the turning points in their lives for light to help us should we meet similar opportunities and crises. The thirteen studies may, however, be stepping-off points for a personal and far more exhaustive study of their lives.

May these studies be a blessing to all who read them. Already, according to reports, God has used them to inspire some of the many thousands who heard them in an original but different form over "The Bible Study Hour."

In spiritual affairs no man can be great in himself. But all can be great in God's service—great, that is, if they humble themselves before God and determine to advance in the way, and only in that way, that God sets before them.

PART ONE

Abraham
The Greatest Patriarch

THE MAN GOD STARTED WITH

(GENESIS 11:27–12:4)

Apart from Jesus Christ, Abraham is probably the most important person in the Bible. Abraham is a giant in Scripture—his stature is far greater than that of Moses, David, or Paul. These latter three were great men, and God used them in great ways, even giving portions of the Scriptures to us through them. But each of them would have agreed without qualification that Abraham was his father in faith.

In the early chapters of Genesis, we read of God's promise to Abraham that he would be the father of many nations (Gen. 17:4). This was fulfilled physically and spiritually. On the physical side, Abraham became the father of the Jewish people, through whom the Messiah was born; he became the father of the many Arab tribes through his son Ishmael. On the spiritual side, Abraham has become the father of a great host of believers whose numbers are now swelled by Christians of countless tongues and nations.

No one can understand the Old Testament without understanding Abraham, for in many ways the story of redemption begins with God's call to this patriarch. Abraham was the first man chosen by God for a role in the plan of redemption. The story of Abraham contains the first mention in the Bible of God's righteousness imputed to man as the sole means of salvation (Gen. 15:6). Matthew includes the genealogy of Jesus in his Gospel in order to trace the beginnings of salvation back to Abraham (Matt. 1:1). Luke declares that the birth of Jesus occurred in response to God's promise to Abraham (Luke 1:68, 72-73).

Great sections of the New Testament explain the spiritual significance of Abraham. An entire chapter in Romans refers to God's dealings with Abraham to support the doctrine of justification by grace through faith (chap. 4). Two chapters in Galatians refer to the life of Abraham to prove that salvation is apart from works (chaps. 3 and 4). One of the longest paragraphs on faith in the Book of Hebrews is devoted to the life of faith lived by this Hebrew patriarch (Heb. 11:8-19). Faith stands preeminent in the life of Abraham.

No Good in Abraham

It is impossible to understand Abraham's faith without realizing that there was nothing in Abraham that commended him to God. God does not look down from heaven to find a person who has a bit of divine righteousness or a bit of faith and then say, "Oh, isn't it wonderful! I've found somebody with a bit of faith. I think I'll save him." When God looks down from heaven He sees that all men are without faith, and He passes a universal judgment: "They are all gone out of the way, they are together become unprofitable; there is none that doeth good, no, not one" (Rom. 3:12). That included Abraham.

This truth is reinforced by another. Abraham came from a family of idol worshipers, and was undoubtedly an idol worshiper himself. This truth is clearly stated in at least three places in the Bible.

THE MAN GOD STARTED WITH

In the last chapter of the Book of Joshua, the aging leader delivers a final spiritual charge to the people of Israel. Joshua begins by reminding them of their pagan past. "Thus saith the Lord God of Israel, Your fathers dwelt on the other side of the river [the River Euphrates] of old, even Terah, the father of Abraham, and the father of Nahor; and they served other gods. And I took your father, Abraham, from the other side of the river, and led him throughout all the land of Canaan, and multiplied his seed, and gave him Isaac. . . . Now, therefore, fear the Lord, and serve Him in sincerity and in truth; and put away the gods which your fathers served on the other side of the river, and in Egypt" (Josh. 24:2-3, 14). The passage is a black-and-white statement of the fact that Abraham was chosen by God from the midst of a pagan ancestry and that he and Terah had once worshiped false gods.

The same thing is said by Isaiah: "Hearken to Me, ye that follow after righteousness, ye that seek the Lord; look unto the rock from which ye are hewn, and to the hole of the pit from which ye are digged. Look unto Abraham, your father, and unto Sarah, who bore you" (Isa. 51:1-2). The whole thrust of these verses is that there was nothing in the ancestry of the Jewish people that could commend them to God.

The third passage that reveals the truth about Abraham's ancestry is a story from the life of Abraham's grandson, Jacob. Jacob was a schemer—even his name means "supplanter"— and his underhandedness made his brother angry enough to want to kill him. Jacob was forced to flee for his life. Where was he to go? Jacob did what many people do when they are cast adrift by life—he went back to his roots. For Jacob, that was in Mesopotamia, the place from which his grandfather Abraham had come. There Jacob associated himself with his uncle Laban. In time, he married both of Laban's daughters, Leah and Rachel, and came to own a large share of the family's sheep and cattle.

As time passed, bad feelings arose between Jacob and Laban. Jacob decided to return to the land of Canaan, choosing a moment when Laban was away on business. When Laban returned, his nephew, his daughters, and much of the property were gone. The household gods also were missing. Laban set out in pursuit. When he overtook the band that Jacob was leading, he chided Jacob for this action and accused him of having stolen the idols. A search was made but the idols were not found. Jacob's wife, Rachel, who had stolen them, had hidden them in her camel's saddle. This story in Genesis 31 shows that Abraham's relatives still owned and cherished idols at least three generations after God had called Abraham out of Mesopotamia.

God's Choice

It was Abraham whom God chose to be the father of many nations. *But why did God save Abraham?* The answer is simply that this was God's will. In Deuteronomy 7, Moses tells why God chose Israel to be the nation through which He gave the Law and would one day send the Saviour. We read, "The Lord did not set His love upon you, nor choose you, because ye were more in number than any people; for ye were the fewest of all people. But because the Lord loved you . . ." (vv. 7-8).

Why did God love them? Because He loved them. Why did He choose them? Because He chose them. This is not human logic; it is divine logic. It is the logic of grace.

This is the way God loved Abraham, and the way God loves us. We are like Abraham. There is nothing in us to commend us to God. And yet God loves us. Just as He sought Abraham, He seeks to draw us into fellowship with Himself.

In the first chapter of the Gospel of John, the apostle tells how Jesus had come to His own people, the Jews, but they had not received Him. And yet some did—both Jews and Gentiles—and John writes that Christ gave to all who believed authority to become the children of God.

As John wrote these words, however, he seemed to know that some would say, "But, you see, God gave them authority to become children of God because they had faith within; it was because they believed." Lest someone retain a false impression, John adds quickly that these "were born, not of blood, nor of the will of the flesh, nor of the will of man, but of God" (John 1:13). John knew that no Christian ever made the first move toward God; he knew that salvation originates in heaven.

This is unpopular teaching, and men and women have always hated it. They hated it when Isaiah reminded them that nothing in their ancestry commended them to God (see Isa. 51:1-2). They hated it in Christ's day. We are told that from the time Jesus began to teach that "no man can come unto Me, except it were given unto him of My Father, . . . many of His disciples went back, and walked no more with Him" (John 6:65-66). People hate it when this Gospel is preached in our own 20th century. And yet, in spite of the hatred of men, it is true. No man ever seeks God.

God's Call

Abraham's faith was preceded by God's call. God called him when he was without faith and promised to bless him. As a result of this encounter, Abraham believed God and set out on the journey to Canaan. Actually, the call to Abraham came twice, once when he was in Ur of the Chaldees (Acts 7:2-4), and once, years later, when he was in Haran.

The Bible says, "Now the Lord had said unto Abram, 'Get thee out of thy country, and from thy kindred, and from thy father's house, unto a land that I will show thee; and I will make of thee a great nation, and I will bless thee, and make thy name great; and thou shalt be a blessing. And I will bless them that bless thee, and curse him that curseth thee: and in thee shall all families of the earth be blessed.' So Abram departed, as the Lord had spoken unto him" (Gen. 12:1-4). Abraham's departure from Ur was the first evidence of his faith in God and in God's promises.

What is faith? Faith is simply belief, and all men have the capacity for it. They demonstrate it every day of their lives. *Saving* faith is believing God and acting upon that belief. Abraham had saving faith because he believed God when God revealed Himself, and he acted upon his belief by setting out for Canaan immediately.

There are many mistaken views of faith. One links faith to credulity. This is the view that faith is belief without evidence. But God provides evidence, and He does so overwhelmingly. In Abraham's case the evidence was an appearance of God so striking that it got the patriarch and all his family and possessions moving out of their homeland into a land which they had never seen. In our case, the evidence is the biblical account of the life, death, and resurrection of Jesus Christ.

In the way that God called Abraham, God calls all who become His children. God comes to us when we are hopelessly lost in sin and without knowledge of Him (Eph. 2:1-7). This is a universal fact in the spiritual biography of Christians. God's call comes first. And our response is nothing more than belief in God and in His promises.

Perhaps someone says, "Well, that may be right theoretically, but I just *can't* believe."

I disagree. You believe men, don't you? Every time you keep an appointment, sign a contract, ride a bus, read the newspaper, or do anything that involves other people, you show faith in some person, sometimes one whom you have not even met.

In the same way, you can believe God. He is more trustworthy. The Bible says, "If we receive the witness of men, the witness of God is greater" (1 John 5:9). What does God ask us to believe? He asks us to believe that we are lost without Him and that He has done everything through the death and resurrection of the Lord Jesus Christ to save us both for this life and for the life to come.

When Faith Is Weak

Someone may say, "Oh, I am able to believe in the sense that you have been explaining, but my faith is weak. I could become a Christian, but I am afraid that if I do—if I start out with God as Abraham did—I'll falter." Of course you will falter. But salvation depends not on the strength of your faith but on God's overwhelming faithfulness to you.

Abraham faltered. When he was in Ur of the Chaldees, God called Abraham to go to Canaan. Ur was in the Mesopotamian river valley, east of the great Arabian desert. Canaan was west of the desert and bordered the Mediterranean Sea. To obey God's call, Abraham had to leave Ur, travel north along the great Euphrates River, cross the northern end of the Arabian desert, and pass down along the Lebanese highlands, entering Canaan from the north. Abraham began the 1,000-mile journey in the best of faith. And yet, at the end of Genesis 11, we find that Abraham stopped at Haran, a little town in Syria hundreds of miles from Ur but still several hundred miles from Canaan.

Abraham stayed at Haran until his father died. When Abraham started once again for Canaan, he was 75 years old. Was Abraham strong in faith? Not at this point in his life. But God's promises were not withdrawn.

ORDINARY MEN CALLED BY GOD

From God's point of view, the years in Haran were wasted. Abraham learned no new lessons there. And that happens to us. Times come when we stop and sit down spiritually. We must not sit too long. We must confess the emptiness of such moments, yield to God's repeated calls, and let Him lead us into all the blessings He originally intended.

The Second Call

God had called Abraham once and he obeyed. Then Abraham disobeyed and stopped at Haran. Years later God came again, calling, "Get thee out of thy country, and from thy kindred, and from thy father's house, unto a land that I will show thee; and I will make of thee a great nation, and I will bless thee, and make thy name great; and thou shalt be a blessing" (Gen. 12:1-2). God called Abraham a second time, and He calls us a second time also. God always persists in His calling.

This truth is found many places in Scripture. It is found in the story of David. God called David to be the political and moral leader of Israel, but David fell into sin. He stayed in Jerusalem instead of participating in a battle. While in Jerusalem he saw Bathsheba, enticed her, and made love to her. When he learned that she had become pregnant, he attempted to cover his sin by having her husband killed. And yet, God did not cast off King David. Instead He came to him through Nathan to expose his sin and lead him to repentance (2 Sam. 12). God came a second time to David.

When God first called Jonah, He said, "Arise, go to Nineveh, that great city, and cry against it; for their wickedness is come up before Me" (Jonah 1:2). Jonah lived in Galilee near Cana, and the way to Nineveh was east. Did Jonah go east? No, Jonah went *west!* The Bible tells us that Jonah rose up to flee to Tarshish, for which he sailed from the Jewish port of Joppa (Jonah 1:3).

20

At this point in the action, God sent a storm. Jonah ordered himself to be thrown overboard by the sailors. He was swallowed by a great fish and was later vomited out on dry land. He was on the shore, right back where he started, when God came to him to repeat His original commission, "And the word of the Lord came unto Jonah the second time" (Jonah 3:1). These are the most beautiful words in the entire story: ". . . the Lord came unto Jonah the second time."
So it will be with us. The word of the Lord comes to us once, twice, and, if need be, a hundred or a thousand times. He calls us to follow Him. We are so prone to stop. We have many Harans, Bathshebas, or ships to Tarshish. And yet, God calls again and again.

God's Faithfulness

Where do you stand? It may be that you have never responded to God's call the first time. If God is prodding you to believe, if you feel unhappy as you are, if you are looking for something better in life, if you are questioning the truths of Christianity, this is God's working. You must yield to Him. You must trust Him.

Perhaps you have stopped at some place in your walk with God. Perhaps God has given you a command to do something and you have put it off, a step to take and you have refused. You prefer to be where you are. The fullness of blessing is never going to come to you until you obey God and do what He has set before you. You will never improve on His instructions.

Perhaps you are one to whom the Lord is now coming a second time. Take great joy in that. Respond to Him. And rejoice that you serve a God who will not abandon the work that He has once set out to accomplish (see Phil. 1:6).

A SHIELD FOR YOU

(GENESIS 15:1)

Once when I was flying over the Gulf of Mexico on a flight from Mexico City to Philadelphia, I saw the great oil-drilling platforms that rise out of the water off our southern coast. The platforms are man-made islands, large enough to house all the men and machinery necessary to drill for oil under the most adverse conditions. The drilling rigs are often lashed by storms. They are buffeted by immense tides. And yet they are secure because they are built upon three great pilings that reach down through many feet of water to bedrock. Three great legs anchor them to a firm foundation.

The Christian life can be compared to such a platform. You are buffeted by life's storms; the forces of Satan often strain against you. Yet you stand secure, not because of your abilities or strength of character, but because you are anchored to the bedrock of the character of God. What anchors you there? Three great spiritual pilings: God's calling, God's faithfulness, and God's power.

God's call does not depend on human merit. God is faithful even when we are unfaithful. And God's power stands behind

His call and His promises. He is all-powerful. These three things combine to make certain the salvation and present security of every believer. We do not trust in our own ability to weather the storms and tides of this life, but in God.

In our first study, we discussed the first two of these three divine realities as they are illustrated in the life of Abraham. We looked at God's call and at God's faithfulness. Now we look at God's power. The Bible says, "After these things the word of the Lord came unto Abram in a vision, saying, 'Fear not, Abram: I am thy shield, and thy exceedingly great reward' " (Gen. 15:1). In these words God was teaching Abraham that He had power to do what He had promised.

Abraham's Shield

In order to understand what God was saying to Abraham here, it is necessary to look back over the preceding chapter, for the verse is directly related to what has gone before. Genesis 15:1 says it was "after these things" that the word of the Lord came unto Abraham. What things? What is in the 14th chapter?

First, there is the story of Abraham's rescue of his nephew Lot from the kings who had defeated Sodom and the cities allied with it. Some time before the battle that this chapter describes, Abraham and Lot had separated, and Lot had gone to live in Sodom.

Sodom was not the place of God's blessing; hence, Lot and his family had problems there. A time came when four kings from distant Mesopotamia began marauding on the eastern edge of Canaan; eventually they came to make war on Sodom and the nearby cities. Sodom's king and his allies were routed, Sodom was overrun, and Lot, his family, and his possessions were captured.

News of the battle came to Abraham. When he heard that

Lot had been captured, Abraham set out to rescue the family. The Bible says, "And when Abram heard that his brother was taken captive, he armed his trained servants . . . and pursued them unto Dan. And he divided his men against them, he and his servants, by night, and smote them, and pursued them unto Hobah . . . and he brought back all the goods, and also brought again his brother, Lot, and his goods, and the women also, and the people" (Gen. 14:14-16).

At this point, Abraham was in great danger. Here were four powerful kings who had laid waste large areas of the land and carried off spoil from many cities. They had presumably spared Abraham only because he was so insignificant and so far away. Now this nobody had attacked them. He had attacked with a small force, but he had won and recovered the spoil. They must have been furious, and Abraham must have been wondering about the consequences of his heroic rescue of his nephew. But while he was wondering, God came to him with a promise of protection, precisely the promise he needed. God said, "Fear not, Abram: I am thy shield, and thy exceedingly great reward."

With such a shield, Abraham was safer than he would have been had he possessed all the power in Canaan. Abraham was shielded by God.

Whom Do You Trust?

Are you shielded as Abraham was? Is God your shield? Do you trust Him? Many men and women trust other things. They trust the government, or their investments, their friends, family, wealth, or popularity. But these things ultimately disappoint the one who trusts them. If you want a real shield, trust God.

Let us think briefly of some of the things against which God promises to shield the one who trusts Him. First, God promises to shield the believer from his *enemies*. David knew this truth. David had made many enemies. He had welded a nation together, and no one can do that without making enemies. He was threatened by the hostile nations that surrounded Israel, old friends of the former king, factions within his own government, and even by rebels within his immediate family. And yet David knew the protective power of God. He wrote, "The Lord is my rock, and my fortress, and my deliverer, the God of my rock; in Him will I trust: He is my shield, and the horn of my salvation, my high tower, and my refuge, my Saviour" (2 Sam. 22:2-3).

God will be your shield against enemies. You may say, as some people do, "Oh, I don't have any enemies!" That may be true. If it is, then I suspect that you are not bearing a very dynamic witness for the Lord Jesus Christ. For the Gospel hardens some hearts as it melts others, and even Jesus had enemies. But if you do have enemies or if you encounter them for the Gospel's sake in days to come, you may be sure that God will be your shield against them.

Second, God promises to shield the believer against Satan. The Bible tells us that our adversary, the devil, "like a roaring lion walketh about, seeking whom he may devour" (1 Peter 5:8). But it also speaks of deliverance. "Submit yourselves, therefore, to God. Resist the devil, and he will flee from you" (James 4:7).

The truth of these verses is illustrated by the story of Job. Job was a righteous man who was severely attacked by Satan. He lost sons and daughters, flocks, camels, asses, yet he did not yield to Satan. The main point of the story is that God had placed a hedge around Job. There was nothing that Satan could do to him until God permitted the hedge to be lowered a little in order to demonstrate Job's character, and God did this only with the full knowledge that Job would triumph and that all that Job had lost would be restored.

God will do that with you also. God will be your shield not only against your enemies but also against Satan, the greatest enemy of all. There is nothing that Satan will ever be able to do to you that will not come first of all through the will of God who allows it in order to bring about a spiritual victory.

Third, God is our shield against *temptation*. Paul writes, "There hath no temptation taken you but such as is common to man; but God is faithful, who will not permit you to be tempted above that ye are able, but will, with the temptation, also make a way to escape, that ye may be able to bear it" (1 Cor. 10:13).

This verse says two things. The first is that no temptation is ever going to come into your life that is too strong for you. God promises that you will only experience temptations that you are able to overcome if you will rest upon Him. Are you tempted by sex, by a chance to be dishonest and escape detection, by a cutthroat way to achieve promotion, by an occasion to gossip? If you are, God knows that, and He knows that you can bear that temptation. You must say, "Lord, I claim Your promise that no temptation that will come to me is beyond my overcoming it. Help me overcome it through Your strength and show me the way of deliverance." And God will help you overcome it.

The second thing that Paul says about temptation is that God always makes a way to escape, that we may be able to bear it. The trouble with most of us is that we do not look for the way to escape. Instead we become fascinated by the temptation, like the bird fascinated by the snake that is about to devour it, and we fail to see God's deliverance. Do you do that? If so, you need to get out of the habit. Learn to look for God's deliverance. Then your life will go on from strength to strength, and you will realize that God is your shield against temptation also.

Finally, God is our shield against *bitterness*. In Philippians

1:12, Paul wrote that the suffering he endured actually served to advance the Gospel. For that he was rejoicing.

A woman in Washington, D.C., told me a similar story. She and her husband had been missionaries to Pakistan but had been sent home suddenly in the midst of one term. They settled in Portsmouth, Virginia, and had not been there long when a gang of youths led by a 14-year old and a 17-year-old boy attacked their young son. The boy was struck about the face and neck with a nail-studded rope and was left 90 percent blinded in his left eye and with no central vision in his right eye. About half-normal vision was later restored to his right eye.

In time, the boys involved were tried and sentenced by the courts. Throughout the course of the trial, the parents of the injured boy refused to give way to bitterness or to indulge their feelings of disappointment. They gave a Christian witness to the offenders. The mother told the newspapers, "If necessary, we can live with a physical handicap. But we can't live with bitterness."

She told me of her many opportunities to speak of Christ's love and power, and said that she trusted the Lord to spread the Gospel through such suffering. In the same way, God can be your shield against bitterness.

Abraham's Reward

But divine protection is only half of the story of God's promise to Abraham. God said, "Fear not, Abram: I am thy shield." He also said, "And thy exceedingly great reward." For the meaning of that phrase, turn to the second half of Genesis 14.

When Abraham returned from the battle against the four kings (recorded in the first half of the chapter), he met Melchizedek, the king of Salem. Salem was probably the ancient city of Jerusalem. Melchizedek was a king and a priest of the most high God. We know that Abraham had great respect for him, for he gave Melchizedek tithes of the spoils of the battle. Abraham returned the rest of the spoils to the king of Sodom. Now, in ancient times the spoils of a battle were the warrior's reward. They were a badge of his daring and success. Abraham had every right to keep the spoils that he had brought back from the battle, but he forfeited them. And as he was standing again in Hebron with his servants, just as he was before the battle, God came to him and said, "Fear not, Abram: I am . . . thy exceedingly great reward."

That is a great promise. God Himself was Abraham's reward. And He is your reward also. Do you seek for things? Do you think that your reward consists of things you can earn? or do? or know? If so, you will certainly be disappointed. These things will all pass away. Let God be your reward, for God will never pass away.

All That God Has

To have God as your reward means, first of all, that you share in all that God has. Abraham received many revelations from God during his lifetime, and many of these revelations had a name of God connected with them. Abraham had come to know God as Jehovah, whose name means *I Am That I Am.* Later he came to know Him as Jehovah-jireh, *the God who provides.* In this story he comes to know Him as El Elyon, *the most high God,* possessor of heaven and earth. It was this God who promised to be a reward to Abraham. God possesses heaven and earth, and all that God has He will share with those who trust Him.

He will share it with you, if you are a believer in the Lord Jesus Christ. The Bible says that we are children of God "and if children, then heirs—heirs of God, and joint heirs with Christ" (Rom. 8:17). You are God's heir. There is a great difference between an heir and a joint heir. If you are a single heir, you alone inherit everything. If you are one of four heirs, then you receive only one-fourth of the inheritance. If, however, you are one of four joint heirs, you inherit all, for joint heirs possess the inheritance together. In the same way, all Christians are joint heirs with Christ. All that God has is ours. We possess it jointly. And we shall enter into it one day as we receive our inheritance with Jesus.

All That God Is

To have God as your reward also means that you share in all that God is. You possess it in part even now. There is hardly an attribute of God mentioned in the Bible that is not said in some verse to be ours in Christ Jesus. Is God wisdom? We share that wisdom. Is God holy? We share that holiness. Is God almighty? We share that power. Paul wrote, "I can do all things through Christ, who strengtheneth me" (Phil. 4:13). And he speaks of Jesus "who of God is made unto us wisdom, and righteousness, and sanctification, and redemption" (1 Cor. 1:30). God Himself is our reward. And having Him we have all.

How do you live your life as a Christian? You can live it in either of two ways. You are already secure in God, more secure even than the oil rigs off the southern coast, for you are anchored in God's character. And you have a great inheritance. But you can either rest in that or be fearful. You can sit on the platform and watch the storms come and say, "Oh, what if the thing falls over? What will become of me then? What if I prove unfaithful?" Or you can be like Abraham and grow strong in faith, resting in Him who is able to keep you from falling and to present you faultless before His presence with exceeding joy. Is your faith like that? If it is not, God can teach you. Then you will grow strong in faith, giving glory to God. You will learn that what God has promised He is able to perform.

PROMISES TO LIVE BY

(GENESIS 15 and 17)

A number of years ago a person said to me, "I never believe anything just because someone has said it." But in a few minutes he hurried off to see someone who had promised to meet him in half an hour on the other side of town. Obviously, whether we admit it or not, we often do things because of another's promise, and would be abnormal if we didn't.

Have you ever noticed how many things in your life depend on someone's promise? You enter into business, get married, buy a piece of property, and do a thousand other things because of someone's promise.

If you are a Christian, you act on the promises of God. Because of His promises you believe that your sins are forgiven, that you possess eternal life, that God hears prayer, that God will provide for you in this life, and that you move toward a blessed existence in the life to come. And you live accordingly. Because promises play such a crucial role in daily life, the nature of God's promises to us is of great importance.

Much in the story of Abraham deals with God's promises. In chapters 15 and 17 of Genesis, God states His promises to

Abraham, dramatizes them by a covenant, and confirms them by the institution of a sign. The covenant itself is mentioned 12 times in chapter 17 alone. And the terms of the covenant define the nature of God's promises not only to Abraham but also to the Jewish people and to all who are the children of Abraham by faith.

What is a covenant? It is simply a promise—in this case, a promise made by God to Abraham. "Promise" is really a better word, for the word "covenant" suggests a bargain, and God's covenants are established apart from the bargaining capacities of men. What are the characteristics of God's promises? First, they are unilateral; they are established by God alone. Second, they are eternal and irrevocable. And third, they are always based on grace, because no man deserves the promises that God makes to him. These three points are illustrated in the story of Abraham.

A One-Sided Covenant

Abraham had been bothered for years by the fact that he had never given life to a son. Abraham was an Oriental, and the ability to procreate children was greatly admired in his culture. Children were even considered a sign of favor with God. Abraham wanted a son for this reason. Then, too, a son was connected with the promise. God had promised Abraham that he was to be the father of a great nation, that the nation would inherit Canaan, and that blessing would come to all nations through his posterity (Gen. 12:1-3; 15:7; 17:1-8).

Certainly there could be no such inheritance or blessing apart from the birth of a son. God had given the promise. Now Abraham asked for a sign that would ratify it.

We must remember at this point that an oath is confirmed in different ways in different societies. In America, if you are in court and you swear to tell the truth, the whole truth, and nothing but the truth, you confirm your oath by placing your hand on a Bible. In the office of a notary public, you may be asked to confirm an oath by raising your hand. In Muslim lands, an oath is confirmed by reference to the beard of the prophet (Muhammad).

But in Abraham's day an oath was confirmed by a ceremony in which animals were cut into two parts along the backbone and placed in two rows, the rows facing each other across a space marked off between them. The parties to the oath walked together into the space between the parts and spoke their promises there. The oath was especially sacred because of the shed blood, and violation of it was considered great dishonor.

It was this ceremony which God enacted with Abraham. In the case of Abraham, however, God alone passed between the pieces (Gen. 15:17). Abraham was not allowed to participate. When God came to confirm His covenant with Abraham, He confirmed it all by Himself. That is why Hebrews says, referring to the event, "For when God made promise to Abraham, because He could swear by no greater, He swore by Himself, saying, Surely, blessing I will bless thee, and multiplying I will multiply thee. And so, after he had patiently endured, he obtained the promise" (Heb. 6:13-15).

God's Presence

The presence of God in this ceremony was signified by two symbols that were intended to tell Abraham—and us—something of God's nature. First, Abraham saw a "smoking furnace" pass between the animal pieces. In our day we have almost lost the significance of this object, but it was well known in ancient times. It was a small furnace used to purify metal. As the ore was heated within the furnace, the dross separated from the metal and rose to the top. It was the refiner's work to skim off the dross until the metal appeared. He looked into the smoking furnace until he could see his face in the surface of the molten metal. Peter had such a furnace in mind when he wrote of the trial of our faith by fire "being much more precious than of gold that perisheth" (1 Peter 1:7). And Malachi wrote that God "shall sit like a refiner and purifier of silver; and He shall purify the sons of Levi, and purge them like gold and silver, that they may offer unto the Lord an offering in righteousness" (Mal. 3:3). Malachi meant that God refines His people until He can see His image in them.

God wishes to do the same with you. At times the trial may be painful and you may resent the fire. But it will be good for you, for God will purify you until you reflect His image.

The second symbol seen by Abraham was a lamp. The story states that "a burning lamp . . . passed between those pieces" (Gen. 15:17). This, too, is a symbol of God's presence. "God is light, and in Him is no darkness at all" (1 John 1:5). God often presented Himself to His people as light. He appeared as light on Sinai, and the glory transmitted itself to the face of Moses. God appeared in light to Paul on the road to Damascus. Light spoke of the divine presence as the angels appeared to the shepherds in the fields of Bethlehem. It was thus that God appeared to Abraham. God alone moved between the pieces and guaranteed the promises.

An Eternal Covenant

The covenant was not only unilateral—it was also eternal. God's promises are always eternal. They are unchangeable. When God says that He will do a thing, He does not change His mind.

This is indicated in two ways by what God did with Abraham. First, God instituted the rite of circumcision. This is recorded in Genesis 17. If there is any one outstanding thing that you can say about circumcision, it is that it is permanent. The child knew nothing of the rite when he was circumcised. He was not able to say, "I am a Jewish baby, and I elect to be circumcised." But the circumcision was done and the results were permanent. The child may have grown up to hate being Jewish. He may have left his home and his homeland. But wherever he may have gone, the mark of his nationality went with him. It is a sign of the fact that God establishes His covenants forever.

The second indication that the promises are eternal is this. When God spoke His words of promise concerning the land that Abraham and his seed were to inherit, He used the past tense of the verb *to give*. If we were speaking, we would say, "And unto your seed *I will give* this land." God did not speak in this way. He spoke as though the thing were already accomplished. He said, "Unto thy seed *have I given* this land, from the river of Egypt unto the great river, the river Euphrates" (Gen. 15:18).

God also uses the past tense with us. He says that Christ *has borne* our griefs and *carried* our sorrows, that He *has removed* our sin. Does that include only the sin that is past? No. It includes the sin that we have not yet committed. That, too, is past history in God's sight. It is wonderful to know that in God's sight our sin has been dealt with forever, and that His promise of forgiveness is eternal.

God's Promises to Israel

Scripture everywhere testifies to the past and future fulfillment of God's promises to Abraham on behalf of His people.

About 400 years passed after the death of the patriarch Abraham, and the people of Israel were in bondage. They were in Egypt, several millions of them. But God raised up

Moses and worked through him to effect a supernatural deliverance. Even in Egypt, God did not cast off His people. The nation came to Sinai. Here they received the Law and, with it, the institution of the great system of sacrifices intended to reveal the way to God when the Law of God was broken. The Law established true worship, outlawed idolatry, instituted the Sabbath Day of rest, and outlined the duties of a man regarding his neighbor. But even as the Law was being given the people were breaking almost every one of the commandments. And yet God did not cast off His people.

The time came when the Promised Land stretched before them, and spies went out to take the measure of the country. The report came back: "The land is prosperous. It is a land of milk and honey. But there are giants, and we cannot take it." The people were frightened and they refused to go forward. Their lack of trust brought judgment. There followed 40 years of wandering in the desert, and yet the time came when God again brought the people to the border of the land of Canaan. God did not cast off His people.

Israel entered Canaan, and for a while God ruled through judges. When the people disobeyed Him and turned to other gods, He brought judgment and they were ruled by the surrounding hostile nations. When they returned to Him, the times of blessing were restored. Nehemiah recounts this period of their history with all its judgments and concludes, "Nevertheless, for Thy great mercies' sake Thou didst not utterly consume them, nor forsake them, for Thou art a gracious and merciful God" (Neh. 9:31). God did not cast off His people.

In time Israel wanted a king to rule over them instead of God. In His displeasure, God gave them King Saul—and all the problems that came with his reign. And yet, in His grace, God later gave them David, and through him established a line from which the Messiah came. God did not cast off His people.

We turn to Revelation 14 and see God's faithfulness projected to the final days of world history. Here are 144,000 Jewish Christians—12,000 from each of Israel's tribes—saved during the final period of persecution on earth. These stand together with the Gentile believers and sing praises to God and to the Lamb. God will not cast off His people.

The Covenant of Grace

Just as God made a covenant with Abraham and kept it through the years of history, so He has made a covenant with all those who are Christians. He will keep that covenant through all the years of our lives on this earth and throughout eternity. Men are unfaithful. Human beings have nothing to commend themselves to God. If God had not come unilaterally to establish His covenant, none would have believed. If God had not made His covenant eternal, as He is eternal, all would fall away and be lost, for all are variable. If His covenant had not been entirely by grace, none would have heard the promises, for no man deserves them.

But the sovereign, eternal, gracious God did come to establish His covenant, and He confirmed it not with the blood of animals but with the blood of His own Son, Jesus Christ our Lord. During the three hours of darkness when Jesus hung upon the cross, God moved in the darkness to ratify the covenant. And because of Christ's death, we shall never perish—neither shall any man snatch us out of His hand.

A Christian should never let anyone tell him that his security comes from the strength of his faith, his faithfulness in attending church, his baptism, reading the Bible, or whatever it may be. If a Christian fails to do these things, he will suffer for it, and God may subject him to discipline. But salvation does not depend on these. It depends upon God, who in His great grace has established an eternal and unchangeable covenant with His people.

CHAPTER FOUR

THE STEPS
OF FAITH

(GENESIS 17 AND 22)

Several years ago when I was in France I climbed a mountain near the little town of Mans in the province of Isère. It really was not much of a mountain—more like a high hill in the foothills of the Alps—but it was fairly steep, especially near the top. It was a good mountain for a beginner to learn on. The Protestants in the area called the mountain Calvin's Bonnet because it looks like a hat.

Early in the morning my friends and I took our first steps along the road that gradually led up the mountain. By midmorning the way had become steeper. As we drew near the summit, the rise became abrupt, and at last we had to work our way up the side of a precipice. Of course, once we reached the top, the view of the higher Alps was splendid and we congratulated ourselves on our efforts.

The Upward Call

The walk of faith is like that. The steps of faith lead uphill, but they begin gradually because our faith starts small. At first the incline is gradual; the climb is easy. But God has arranged the route so that the way becomes harder and the faith of the climber is inevitably strengthened with each step of his journey. We may wish that the way were less difficult. But it is only through the difficult climbing that anyone reaches the heights. And only from the peak can we see the panorama of God's best plans for us and His purposes in history.

That is what happened to Abraham. At first Abraham's faith was a very simple thing; it meant only believing in God's call and doing what God told him to do (Gen. 12:1). But God soon led him to higher ground; he was asked to believe that God could give him a son when he was past the age of engendering children and Sarah was past the years of fertility (Gen. 17:16-17). At this point, faith in God meant believing that God was able to perform a miracle. Abraham believed that God could do it, and he was not disappointed. In that step Abraham learned to recognize God as the God of the impossible. And he grew strong in faith, giving God the glory.

God of the Impossible

Apart from the appearance of God to Abraham, first in Ur of the Chaldees and later in Haran, nothing in the story of Abraham before Genesis 17 has anything to do with the miraculous. With chapter 17, this changes. Abraham was 86 years old when his concern for a son had last been shared with God. Abraham was now 99 years old (v. 1). At this point Abraham was hoping that Ishmael, who had been born in his old age of a slave girl, might be blessed as the son of God's promise (v. 18).

The natural birth of Ishmael was not of God's doing, however, and in time God came again to Abraham. He reiterated the promise of a son through Sarah: "Behold, My covenant is with thee, and thou shalt be a father of many nations. Neither shall thy name any more be called Abram, but thy name shall be Abraham; for a father of many nations have I made thee. And I will make thee exceedingly fruitful, and I will make nations of thee, and kings shall come out of thee" (Gen. 17:4-6). This was the promise that God made to Abraham, and its fulfillment now required a special miracle.

What did Abraham do? The Bible tells us that Abraham "was strong in faith, giving glory to God" and was "fully persuaded that, what He had promised, He was able also to perform" (Rom. 4:20-21). In the following year Sarah gave birth to Isaac, who was the son of promise and an ancestor of the Lord Jesus Christ.

Do you have a faith like that? A God like that? The God we worship is the God of Abraham, and this God works in men to bring forth faith like Abraham's. This God brings life out of death, love out of hate, peace out of turmoil, joy out of misery, praise out of cursing, and miracles to those who trust Him. In our day He does so through Jesus Christ who is the focal point and ultimate heir of the promises.

The final step on the path of Abraham's faith appears in Genesis 22. God put Abraham to a severe test, and Abraham learned something about God's dealings with men that he would have learned in no other way. God said, "Take now thy son, thine only son Isaac, whom thou lovest, and get thee into the land of Moriah; and offer him there for a burnt offering upon one of the mountains which I will tell thee of" (Gen. 22:2). Abraham obeyed God. I believe that through this test Abraham learned something about the coming of Jesus Christ and entered into the very mind of His heavenly Father.

Faith in Crisis

The test that came to Abraham was, first of all, a test of his devotion to God. Was God to be everything to Abraham? Or was something else—perhaps even God's gift of Isaac—to come between them?

We must remember that Abraham was 86 years old when he had his first son by Hagar. He was 100 years old when Sarah at last gave birth to Isaac. Now Isaac had become a young man, perhaps 15 years of age, and Abraham was probably about 115 years old. Abraham had loved this son from birth, as any father would. This love had grown strong over the years in which Abraham had seen Isaac grow to young manhood. He loved him not only because he was the son of his old age, the result of a miracle, but also because he was the son of the promise.

We can only begin to imagine the depth of the struggle in Abraham's heart during the long night in which he wrestled with the thought of losing Isaac. But whatever the struggle was, and however deep it was, it was all over by the following morning. The Abraham that emerged in the morning was an Abraham committed to obedience. The story says, "And Abraham rose up early in the morning, and saddled his ass, and took two of his young men with him, and Isaac his son, and cut the wood for the burnt offering, and rose up, and went unto the place of which God had told him" (Gen. 22:3). Abraham had not put the gift ahead of the Giver.

But the test was not only a test of Abraham's devotion to God; it was also a test of his spiritual perception. Think of the things Abraham had learned in the years before Isaac's birth. At one time he had been tempted to think that God would not keep His promises and that a household servant would be his legal heir (Gen. 15:2). But God had taught him that the blessing would not come through the household servant.

42

THE STEPS OF FAITH

Abraham later wanted to substitute Ishmael, the son of Hagar, for Isaac, before Isaac was born (Gen. 17:18). But God had taught him that the blessing would not come through the son of the Egyptian slave girl. God had taught Abraham that the blessing was to come through Isaac, and now God had asked the patriarch to kill Isaac.

We can imagine the troubled reasoning that must have stirred the mind of Abraham in the dark hours of that desert evening. He must have thought something like this: "I know that Isaac is the son of God's promise, and God has shown me time and again that He will not send the blessing through another. And yet, this same God tells me to sacrifice him, to put him to death. How can this be? If I put him to death, as God has commanded, how can God fulfill His promise? How can God do it?"

The puzzle was real. But then, as Abraham wrestled with this supreme test of God's logic, it must have occurred to him (perhaps as the sun was rising) that the God who had done a miracle in bringing about Isaac's birth was also capable of doing a miracle in bringing him back from the dead. This was the solution that his aching heart discovered during the long desert night. And as Abraham started for the mountain in the morning, he must have been saying quietly to himself, "Come on, boy, we are going to see a miracle. God has asked me to sacrifice you on Mount Moriah. But if God is going to be faithful to His promise, He is going to have to raise you up again from the dead. We are going to see a resurrection."

In at least two places the Bible reveals that this is the way it happened. The first is in the story itself. Abraham had come to the foot of the mountain with the boy, and he was ready to go on without the young men who were with him. As he took the kindling and Isaac and prepared to climb the mountain, Abraham said to the others, "Abide ye here with the ass; and I and the lad will go yonder and worship, and come again to you" (Gen. 22:5). Think of that: *and come again to you.* Who would come? Abraham and Isaac! And what does that mean? It means that although Abraham believed that he was going to perform the sacrifice, he also believed that God was going to perform a resurrection and that he would be able to come back down the mountain with his boy.

The second proof is Hebrews 11:17-19, which is the full New Testament commentary on the incident: "By faith Abraham, when he was tested, offered up Isaac; and he that had received the promises offered up his only begotten son, of whom it was said, 'In Isaac shall thy seed be called'; accounting that God was able to raise him up, even from the dead, from which also he received him in a figure." What does that mean? It means that Abraham looked for a resurrection. And in this expectation he triumphed. Once again Abraham grew strong in faith toward God.

The Real Resurrection

The story of Abraham's struggle does not exhaust the narrative, for all that we have seen up to this point is only what Abraham learned before he ascended Mount Moriah. The climax of the story—and the greatest lesson—comes upon the mountain. The Jewish people have a proverb that says, "In the mountain the Lord will provide." I believe that on the mountain Abraham learned that God would one day provide His Son to die for man's salvation.

The first piece of evidence for this conclusion is found in John 8:56. In that verse Jesus speaks of the knowledge of Himself possessed by Abraham. He says, "Abraham rejoiced to see My day; and he saw it, and was glad." What is intended by this word *see?* On this point commentators on the Gospel of John have long been divided. Some see it as a knowledge of Christ that Abraham had in Christ's day (since

Abraham was alive in paradise). Others see it as a vision of Christ's coming that Abraham had in his own day, some 2,000 years before the actual birth of Jesus. To me there is no question but that the latter interpretation is the correct one. For the context of the verse requires the conclusion, not that Abraham existed after death, but that Christ was preexistent. The argument is that He must have existed in the Old Testament to give a revelation of Himself to Abraham.

If this is true, however, we must ask ourselves to what period of Abraham's life the vision spoken of by Jesus refers. The only part of Abraham's life recorded in the Old Testament to which it can possibly refer is the part we are now studying. For only this could be a vehicle to reveal Christ's coming to earth, His death, and His resurrection.

The second line of evidence that Abraham received a revelation of Christ's coming and death lies in the name of God that embodied what Abraham learned on the mountain. As we saw in an earlier study, God had previously revealed Himself to Abraham by different names. The first was Jehovah, which means *I Am That I Am* (Gen. 12:1). As Abraham had given tithes to Melchizedek, he had learned the name El Elyon (Gen. 14:19). This means *the most high God*, and it identifies God as the possessor of heaven and earth. When Abraham learned that God was able to do that which seemed impossible to men, as he did at the birth of Isaac, he came to know God as El Shaddai, which means *God Almighty* (Gen. 17:1). Now he learned that God was also Jehovah-jireh, *the God who provides* (Gen. 22:14). This name was a true revelation of God's character. And it was not exhausted in this one incident. The name points to the fact that the God who would provide a ram as a substitute for the sacrifice of Isaac would also provide a substitute for the death of all men through Jesus Christ.

Another verse points to this same conclusion. In the letter

to the Galatians, where Paul is arguing that salvation is by faith in Jesus Christ alone, he quotes Genesis 22:18 to prove that the blessing of Abraham was to come, not through Israel as a whole, but through the Messiah who was Abraham's seed: "And in thy seed shall all the nations of the earth be blessed" (see Gal. 3:8, 16). But when was this promise given? Not in Ur of the Chaldees, nor in Haran, nor in connection with the birth of Isaac, but after the experience on the mountain when the patriarch almost sacrificed his son. Certainly the experience itself, the name of God, and the promise all point to the sacrifice that God would make of Jesus.

Actually, all this is dramatized in the story itself. And we cannot doubt that God allowed it to happen in this way as an illustration of what would happen 2,000 years later when God would give His Son on Calvary. Look at what happened. As Abraham started out early in the morning, Isaac was as good as dead, for Abraham was determined to obey the Lord's commandment. For three days they traveled on the way to Mount Moriah—the exact length of time that passed between the death of Jesus and His Easter resurrection. Abraham and the boy reached the mountain. The climb was made. Isaac was bound, and Abraham raised his hand to plunge the knife into his son. It was only at this point that God intervened to provide a substitute, a ram caught in the bushes, and to provide a figure of a far greater and more literal resurrection.

Do you see the parallel? Abraham was only called upon to offer his son. But when the time came for God to offer His Son on Calvary, the hand that was poised above Him fell. God put His own Son to death. Jesus endured the full sufferings of death. For three days He lay in the tomb. And then God effected the resurrection and initiated Christ's triumphs. All this was dramatized for Abraham. And through it he learned to look for Christ's coming. Through *his* suffering, Abraham learned of *God's* suffering. He learned what it meant for God to give His Son on Calvary.

Up from the Lowlands

We have reached the end of the story of Abraham, having followed him through a lifetime of learning to walk by faith. His faith grew by stages, and there is an application in at least one of these stages for everyone. Whatever your position in the life of faith, you are at one point of this journey.

Perhaps you are still in Ur of the Chaldees spiritually. If you are, then God is not yet asking you to believe in His power to do the impossible or to learn anything about His ways through suffering. What God is asking you to believe is that you must leave all that you have and all that you are and walk the path He shows you. This path leads first to Jesus. God wants you to leave your sin, your past, your own planning for your life, even your good opinions of yourself, and follow Jesus (Acts 2:37-38; 16:30-31). He died for you. He lives for you. You must believe in Him. Any journey begins with the first step, and this is the first step of faith.

Perhaps you are at the point that Abraham had reached when he was asked to believe that God could do the impossible. God has asked you to move in a direction in which you see nothing but a high brick wall. It may be a trait of character that you are unable to overcome by yourself. It may be a call to be a missionary or to witness to someone that you feel you will never be able to talk to. It may be a call to a life of service. It may mean that you must forego marriage. It may mean submission to seemingly unthinkable circumstances. If you are in that position, then you must learn that the God who has called you is a God who can do the impossible. You must trust Him to remove the wall in your life. And you must step forward in faith, through the wall if necessary, knowing that He is able to keep those who trust Him (Phil. 4:13).

Perhaps you have come to the point that Abraham reached in the last days of his earthly life. God had given him a test that involved much personal suffering, but God had a purpose in that suffering. Perhaps He is doing that with you. If He is, you should take courage in the fact that He will use it to teach you something about Himself and about His purposes in history (Rom. 8:28).

Do you know testing where your children are concerned? Have you tried to bring them up in the Lord, only to see them go their own way? That involves suffering. But through it you may learn what God feels when we are disobedient children. The Bible says, "As a father pitieth his children, so the Lord pitieth them that fear Him" (Ps. 103:13).

Have you a burden for the lost, someone in your family or among your neighbors? Perhaps God would have you learn what Jesus felt when He cried, "O Jerusalem, Jerusalem, thou that killest the prophets, and stonest them who are sent unto thee, how often would I have gathered thy children together, even as a hen gathereth her chickens under her wings, and ye would not!" (Matt. 23:37)

Perhaps you have known abuse for the Gospel's sake—personal, vindictive, unjust abuse—by your family, your friends, or those with whom you work. God may want you to go through this experience in order to learn about His love and about the depths of His compassion in the face of the contradiction of sinners. "The Lord is gracious, and full of compassion, slow to anger, and of great mercy" (Ps. 145:8). If God has led you this far in the journey of faith, you have begun to scale the heights and to learn that the knowledge of God is far more precious than any material blessing. You are becoming a true friend of God, as Abraham was. And you will not want to exchange the heights of this faith for the lowlands.

PART TWO

Moses

The Greatest Leader

YOUR PLAN OR GOD'S

(EXODUS 2:11-15)

Shortly after the turn of the last century, out in Missouri, a young man enrolled at the State Teachers College in Warrensburg to get an education. He was a poor lad who could not afford to live in town, so he commuted three miles each day by horseback in order to attend classes. He had only one good suit. His coat was too thin. He tried out for the football team and was rejected.

In spite of his obvious pluck and courage, the young student was developing a deep-seated inferiority complex. His mother urged him to do something that would demonstrate his real potential, so he tried public speaking. Unfortunately, he failed at that too. At this stage in his life, everything the young man did ended in failure.

Yet Dale Carnegie kept on, and eventually became the best-known teacher of public speaking in history. The lad who had failed at speaking became the personal manager of radio's celebrated newscaster and author Lowell Thomas, and developed a course of instruction on "How to Win Friends and Influence People" that made him a millionaire.

It is an old story—a story of initial failure culminating in eventual success—but few, particularly Christians, realize that this is often a Christian story also. We may not like to think so, but Christians do fail. Through their failures they should learn to trust God in order that they might succeed in His service. Another way of saying the same thing is that through failures they learn to follow God's plans for their lives rather than their own.

In this chapter we have just such an example. Have you ever noticed that the first episode in the adult life of Moses ends in total failure? This is remarkable because, as far as we can tell, Moses acted with the highest of motives throughout the incident and was confident that he was performing the will of God.

Moses expected to deliver the Israelites from slavery. He began by defending one of them against unjust oppression. He failed, and ended up by fleeing from Egypt as an outlaw. It was only after Moses had spent the next 40 years as a shepherd on the far side of the desert in Midian—and reached the age of 80—that God appeared to him and called him to the work of bringing the Israelites out of Egypt.

Why did this happen? I believe that God allowed Moses' plans to go awry (among other reasons) that we might be encouraged when the same thing happens to us. Moses was the greatest lawgiver who ever lived. His name is mentioned over 700 times in the Bible. He was used by God in greater ways than any other Old Testament character. If a man can begin his career in such abject failure as Moses experienced and then rise to the heights he achieved, certainly we can rise from our early failures and ruined plans too. If we do not—if we grieve over our plans that seemed good and even spiritual to us but which failed—then we do not understand God's sovereignty. We need to take our minds off our plans for a while and seek God.

Faith in the Home

In order to understand the context of Moses' great decision to help the oppressed members of his race, we need first to understand something of his exceptional training. There is no doubt that the seeds of his greatness were planted and nurtured during the days of his youth and early manhood.

In the first place, Moses received remarkable spiritual training in his home. We must not think that all the people of Israel were faithful to the God of Abraham, Isaac, and Jacob during the years of their oppression. Certainly the majority were not. These were people who would later persuade Moses' elder brother Aaron to make a calf out of their jewelry that they might worship it in the desert. Many had become idol worshipers, as Abraham had been before God called him out of Ur of the Chaldees. Yet some did remain faithful. In their lives and homes, the knowledge of the true God was passed on from parents to children, generation after generation. It was into such a believing family that Miriam, Aaron, and Moses were born.

Moses' father's name was Amram, meaning "an exalted people," and his mother's name was Jochebed, meaning "God is honored" (Ex. 6:20). They were a spiritual couple whose faith, even in hard times, was in the Lord. The Book of Hebrews speaks of their faith: "By faith Moses, when he was born, was hidden three months by his parents, because they saw he was a beautiful child, and they were not afraid of the king's commandment" (Heb. 11:23). The second chapter of Exodus shows their faith in action during the dangerous days of Moses' infancy.

Several factors lead us to think that their faith came to a high pitch when Moses was born and that they probably realized that God had sent him to be the promised deliverer (Gen. 15:13-14). The words used to describe the baby Moses indicate this slightly, for the Hebrew says, "He was a *beautiful child*" (Ex. 2:2). And Stephen, in the New Testament, calls him "exceedingly fair" or "fair unto God" (Acts 7:20). The words imply that there was something exceptional, something significant in his birth.

Then, too, the mother prepared an ark for his deliverance, and this implied faith. No mother who loved her child would willingly trust it to the river unless she believed that God would take care of her little one. If she did not have this faith, she would keep the child at home near herself, even though the soldiers were hunting up and down the streets to destroy the child. The nature of a mother's heart demands it. Yet this mother, Jochebed, placed her child in a basket and set it in the reeds by the river.

Finally, she placed the child's elder sister, Miriam, on the bank to watch and report what happened. Now you do not place a nine-year-old girl on a bank near a river to watch the brutal murder of a baby, if that is what you think might happen. You place her there only if you expect God to deliver the child and want to know about it. This is what Jochebed expected. When the baby was discovered by the daughter of the Pharaoh and later given back to the mother for nursing, Jochebed undoubtedly saw the deliverance and preservation of the child as an example of God's providential working.

It was in a home conditioned by such faith that Moses was reared. And we can be certain that Jochebed shared with Moses the story of his remarkable deliverance. She would have impressed upon him the knowledge that the Hebrew people had of Jehovah; she would have told him of the calling of the patriarchs. And she may have communicated her faith that this same God was going to use Moses himself to lead them to the land of Canaan from the painful bondage of the Egyptians.

Training at Court

In addition to the training received in his home, Moses was heir to a remarkable education in the courts of Pharaoh. God had arranged a first-class secular education for him.

The account in Exodus throws no light on the nearly 40 years Moses spent in the courts of Egypt. But Stephen said that "Moses was learned in all the wisdom of the Egyptians, and was mighty in words and in deeds" (Acts 7:22). That is what we should expect of the education of an adopted son of Pharaoh's daughter. In Moses' day, as for centuries before and after, the land of Egypt was noted for its mastery of the art of written communication. By means of the hieroglyphic and more popular cuneiform systems of writing, Egyptian learning thrived in the second millennium B.C. Heliopolis was a center of scribal and priestly learning. Presumably Moses was instructed in reading and writing, thereby developing the skills that he was to use later in drafting the first five books of the Bible.

Egypt was also noted for its mastery of mathematics, astronomy, architecture, music, and medicine. Its monuments are still recognized among the great wonders of the ancient world. Its mummies have been discovered bearing the marks of dentistry and a primitive form of brain surgery. Presumably Moses mastered part, if not all, of this knowledge and thus brought to the task before him the best training and deepest wisdom of the world. It is no small tribute to his own native wisdom that he willingly remained in the courts of Pharaoh long enough to gain this mastery.

The Choice of Moses

At some point during these long years of preparation—we do not know precisely when—Moses began to develop his plans for delivering his people from the Egyptians. Likely he considered rebelling and using force. In any event, he used force when he saw an Egyptian beating one of the Hebrews; when it was all over, the Egyptian lay dead, buried in the sand (Ex. 2:11-12). Moses' action was selfless, but it was not God's will. The significant point is that Moses' plans were not the same as the plans made by God for the deliverance of the Hebrews.

To say this is not to impugn the moral and spiritual character of Moses. He is praised for this action in at least two places in the New Testament.

Stephen, in his great sermon before the Sanhedrin, acknowledged that it was out of spiritual motives that Moses avenged the persecuted Hebrew by killing the Egyptian: "For he supposed his brethren would have understood how that God by his hand would deliver them" (Acts 7:25).

The author of Hebrews writes, "By faith Moses, when he was come to years, refused to be called the son of Pharaoh's daughter, choosing rather to suffer affliction with the people of God than to enjoy the pleasures of sin for a season, esteeming the reproach of Christ greater riches than the treasures in Egypt, for he had respect unto the recompense of the reward" (Heb. 11:24-26).

On the basis of these verses one author has written in praise of Moses: "Bred in a palace, he espoused the cause of the people; nursed in the lap of luxury, he embraced adversity; reared in the school of despots, he became the champion of liberty; long associated with oppressors, he took the side of the oppressed; educated as her son, he forfeited the favor of a princess to maintain the rights of the poor; with a crown in prospect, he had the magnanimity to choose a cross; and for the sake of his God and Israel, abandoned ease, refinement, luxuries, and the highest earthly honors, to be a houseless wanderer." (Quoted by Arno C. Gaebelein, *Moses—His First*

and Second Coming, Our Hope Publications, New York, N.Y.
No source indicated.)

These things are true. And yet the path that Moses chose
to walk was not God's path. Moses was guilty. "He looked
this way and that" before killing the Egyptian (Ex. 2:12).
And the murder ended in the total destruction of his plans.
The Bible says, "Now when Pharaoh heard this thing, he
sought to slay Moses. But Moses fled from the face of Pharaoh, and dwelt in the land of Midian" (Ex. 2:15). When
Moses returned from that enforced exile years later, he was a
different man, but he was one fit for years of selfless and
obedient service.

God's Plan in Our Failures

Moses' first great choice and failure shows that God's true
servants can sometimes fail miserably. In our failures, we can
gain a measure of encouragement from that. However, Moses' experience also shows that God is able to accomplish His
plans even in the midst of our failures. In fact, He allows our
failures—for He certainly *could* prevent them—in order to
teach us lessons we would never learn if we were constantly
intoxicated with the heady wine of success.

God uses our failures to teach us at least three important
things. The first is that no matter how talented we are, or
may think ourselves to be, without Him we can do nothing.
Jesus said, "I am the vine, ye are the branches. He that
abideth in Me, and I in him, the same bringeth forth much
fruit; for without Me ye can do nothing" (John 15:5).

Unfortunately, most of us do not think this way. If we
acknowledge our inadequacy at all, we acknowledge it with a
qualification that really means, "Without Me ye cannot do
very much." Most of us are like Moses, who thought that his
talents and training were in themselves entirely adequate for

the job. When we think like that, God will often allow us to fail in order to show us that all that is worthwhile is done "not by might, nor by power, but by My Spirit, saith the Lord" (Zech. 4:6).

The second thing God teaches us through our failures is that we are capable of terrible things if we persist in our way instead of proceeding in His way. The things we do become terrible primarily because we seldom stop in our failures until we have made a thorough botch of everything.

This truth may be illustrated by an incident in Paul's life that was remarkably similar to this incident in the life of Moses. Early in his ministry, Paul had conceived a plan for taking up a collection in the Gentile churches to relieve the physical need of the saints in Jerusalem. This was in itself a good thing. But somewhere along the line, Paul's personal desires apparently began to intrude into this noble plan. Paul became proud and perhaps even tyrannical in pursuing it. On one occasion he wrote to the Christians at Corinth mentioning that he had actually ordered the Galatians to take up this collection (1 Cor. 16:1-2). And in the following verses he spoke of leading the procession that would bear the gift to the Jerusalem Christians.

Even at this point we might think Paul's plans were proper and only his methods somewhat questionable. But when we turn to the Book of Acts and read the actual account of his journey, we find that the Holy Spirit made several attempts to stop him. When he arrived at Miletus, Paul spoke of his own spiritual depression, "And now, behold, I go bound in the spirit [not the Holy Spirit] unto Jerusalem, not knowing the things that shall befall me there" (Acts 20:22). When he reached Tyre, the Christians there—inspired by the Holy Spirit—tried to warn him, "And finding disciples, we tarried there seven days; who said to Paul through the Spirit, that he should not go up to Jerusalem" (Acts 21:4). At Caesarea the

Prophet Agabus took Paul's belt, bound his own hands and feet with it, and said, "Thus saith the Holy Spirit, 'So shall the Jews at Jerusalem bind the man that owneth this belt, and shall deliver him into the hands of the Gentiles' " (Acts 21:11).

Finally, the Lord Jesus Christ Himself appeared to Paul in a vision saying, "Make haste, and get thee quickly out of Jerusalem" (Acts 22:18). Yet Paul persisted. Paul had been warned by his feelings, by other Christians, by a prophet of the Lord, and by the Lord Jesus Christ personally. Still he went his way, eventually succumbing to the point of trying to take a Jewish vow. As God had forewarned, he was then arrested, imprisoned, and two years later deported as a prisoner to Rome.

What did Paul learn from this experience? It was probably after all this that he wrote to Timothy: "This is a faithful saying, and worthy of all acceptance, that Christ Jesus came into the world to save sinners, of whom I am chief" (1 Tim. 1:15). Earlier he had called himself the "least of the apostles" (1 Cor. 15:9); then, "less than the least of all saints" (Eph. 3:8). But now, through willful persistence in his own plans, he had learned what terrible actions he was capable of without God.

The final lesson that God can teach us through the failure of our own plans is that He is capable of working for us and in us in spite of us. Only after we fail do we become aware that it is God and not ourselves who is working. God's plans will be accomplished. "There are many devices in a man's heart; nevertheless the counsel of the Lord, that shall stand" (Prov. 19:21). This truth Moses came to know, and we must learn it also. Someone has said, "Moses was 40 years in Egypt learning something; he was 40 years in the desert learning to be nothing; and he was 40 years in the wilderness proving God to be everything."

Have you proved God to be everything? You are a long way toward learning these lessons if you have come to pursue God's plans rather than your own.

CHAPTER SIX

THE BATTLE AGAINST THE GODS

(EXODUS 7–10)

When George Bernard Shaw's *Pygmalion* first appeared on Broadway as the musical *My Fair Lady*, the advertisements showed a design in which Shaw, looking like a cartoonist's version of God, was controlling a puppet that looked like Dr. Higgins, who in turn was controlling a puppet that looked like Eliza. We have a similar situation in the battle that took place in ancient Egypt between God Almighty and the demon gods that stood behind the polytheistic religion of that country.

A historian might look at the records and say, "Moses must have been a great leader, and the victory was his victory. He succeeded in rallying the people to the point at which they were ready to leave Egypt."

Someone less inclined to identify heroes in the records and more disposed to see great historical movements might say, "No, what we have here is not a great genius or leader, but a mass movement of people."

Neither of these would be correct. God tells us that if we will look at the confrontation through spiritual eyes, we shall see that the battle was not only between Israel and Egypt, or between Moses and Pharaoh. The battle pitted Jehovah, the true God, who moved Moses and Israel, against all the false gods of the Egyptian pantheon, backed by a host of fallen angels who had turned from God as a part of Lucifer's original rebellion.

The battle was waged with great intensity. But the result was a total and uncompromising victory for Jehovah. Through that victory the power of Egypt was broken, the people of Israel set free, and a series of stern judgments enacted against the false gods who figure prominently in the deliverance story.

This spiritual perspective on the Exodus may be questioned by some. But it is set forth in a very explicit statement in the Book of Numbers: "These are the journeys of the children of Israel, who went forth out of the land of Egypt with their armies under the hand of Moses and Aaron. . . . And they departed from Rameses in the first month, on the 15th day of the first month; on the next day after the passover the children of Israel went out with an high hand in the sight of all the Egyptians. For the Egyptians buried all their firstborn, which the Lord had smitten among them; upon their gods also the Lord executed judgments" (Num. 33:1-4). The last phrase is a clear statement that the real battle in Egypt was between God, who stood behind Moses, and the gods, who stood behind Pharaoh.

Worship of Satan

It is important to note, as background to the struggle recorded in Exodus 7–12, that the worship of the Egyptian gods was linked to the worship of Satan and to the lesser demons who were associated with him in his fall.

It is natural to think that the polytheism of Egypt was

merely an empty religion—a religion centering in the worship of nothing, a no-god (as the Bible calls idols; see Gal. 4:8)—and hence meaningless. But the Bible says that the battle was to be waged against "all the gods of Egypt" (Ex. 12:12 with Num. 33:4). This implies a real battle against real spiritual forces, and the only forces that can fit this category are demonic ones.

In my own mind I envision the hosts of Satan to be something like the family dog which is always present at the table to catch whatever scraps he can from those eating. The food is not for the dog, but he will get it whenever possible. If the members of the family were weak enough, the dog would eat it all and eventually reduce the family to the point where they would exist only to feed and pamper him.

We know that Satan desires worship. His most audacious utterance to Jesus Christ was, "All these things will I give Thee, if Thou wilt fall down and worship me" (Matt. 4:9).

We know that men refuse to give God worship. We may therefore imagine that whenever a man refuses to give God worship and invents another object to worship, Satan or one of his followers will soon present himself and attempt to turn a sinful, rebellious worship of nothing, of a no-god, into a far more serious and rebellious worship of himself.

That is what happened in Egypt. It was therefore against the principalities and powers that stood behind the outward forms of Egyptian polytheism that the wrath and judgment of Jehovah were directed. He told Moses, "Against all the gods of Egypt I will execute judgment: I am the Lord" (Ex. 12:12). That is precisely what He did.

A Plague on the River

The first of God's judgments was against the waters of Egypt. We read that Aaron lifted up his rod and "smote the waters that were in the river, in the sight of Pharaoh and in the sight of his servants; and all the waters that were in the river were turned to blood. And the fish that were in the river died; and the river stank, and the Egyptians could not drink of the water of the river; and there was blood throughout all the land of Egypt" (Ex. 7:20-21).

We need to picture in our minds what this meant. Egypt owes its entire life to the Nile. If it were not for the river, all Egypt would be desert. From the Nile comes water for irrigation, the primary means of transportation, fertile topsoil, and other things vital to the life of the country. The Nile was then and is still today the most important thing in Egypt.

It follows as a consequence that in a debased polytheism many of the gods would be associated with the life or the functions of the river. Osiris, one of the chief gods of Egypt, was first of all god of the Nile. In Upper Egypt, Hapimon and Tauret were also Nile gods. Nu was the god of life in the river. To these gods, prayers had been addressed and offerings had been made for hundreds and even thousands of years. Now the "divine Nile" became a river of death and putrefaction. The plague lasted seven days. It was a solemn judgment. Nevertheless, at the end of the period the Bible records that Pharaoh's heart was hardened, and he refused to let the people go (Ex. 7:22).

Abundance of Frogs

The second plague that Jehovah brought upon Egypt was one of frogs. God said, "Behold, I will smite all thy borders with frogs: and the river shall bring forth frogs abundantly, which shall go up and come into thine house, and into thy bedchamber, and upon thy bed, and into the house of thy servants, and upon thy people, and into thine ovens, and into thy kneading troughs. And the frogs shall come up both on thee, and upon thy people, and upon all thy servants" (Ex. 8:2-4). That is what happened. Aaron stretched forth his hand over the waters of Egypt and frogs came up out of the waters and covered the land.

If we are to understand the full significance of this plague, we must recognize that a goddess of Egypt was involved in the judgment—the goddess Hekt, who was always pictured with the head and often the head and body of a frog. Since Hekt was embodied in the frog, the frog was sacred in Egypt. It could not be killed, and consequently there was nothing the Egyptians could do about this horrible and ironic proliferation of the goddess. They were forced to loathe the symbols of their depraved worship. But they could not kill them. And when the frogs died, their decaying bodies must have turned the towns and countryside into a stinking horror.

What did Pharaoh do? He hardened his heart, but not before he had done something else. Pharaoh turned to the magicians of Egypt and said to them, "You have lived in Egypt longer than Moses. Can't you conjure up frogs?" So the magicians did. But, of course, that was not the problem. There were plenty of frogs. They did not need more. The problem was to get rid of them. The magicians were not equal to that, however. Finally Pharaoh came to Moses and said, "Entreat the Lord, that He may take away the frogs from me, and from my people; and I will let the people go" (Ex. 8:8). Moses prayed. The frogs died. But after they were removed, Pharaoh again set his mind against the inevitable deliverance.

Plagues on the Land

In ancient times, as now, the soil of Egypt was one of the most fertile soils in the world, thanks to the tons of rich earth carried down the river from the south and deposited in Egypt by the yearly inundation of the Nile. Out of this soil came wonderfully nourishing fruits and vegetables. As part of God's judgment upon the land, and hence upon the earth god (known as Geb), the land was now to bring forth insects and swarms of flies which were to defile the bodies of the people and even prevent the official functions of the priests.

The third plague is commonly referred to as the plague of gnats, or lice. We read, "Aaron stretched out his hand with his rod, and smote the dust of the earth, and it became lice in man and in beast; all the dust of the land became lice throughout all the land of Egypt" (Ex. 8:17).

The exact identification of this insect is unknown. The Greek version of the Old Testament translates the word *skniphes*, which means gnats. The Hebrew uses the word *kinnim*, mentioned by Philo and Origen, which may indicate a form of sand fly or flea that dug beneath the skin and caused a disagreeable itching and pain. Whatever it was, it defiled the bodies of the Egyptians and halted religious activity, for the priests could serve only while their bodies were ceremonially clean.

The fourth plague brought great swarms of flies and other insects over the land. In this case the Hebrew text merely says "swarms," not bothering to specify what insects were involved, and the implication seems to be that all the insects of Egypt increased unnaturally, infesting the streets, the courts, and the homes.

Like earlier plagues, this one brought an infestation of creatures, such as the beetle, which were sacred to the people. They could not be killed. They could only be endured. We do not know how long this plague lasted, but after a time, Pharaoh called for Moses and Aaron and offered to compromise. They could sacrifice to Jehovah, but only in the land of Egypt. However, God did not compromise with him. God demanded unconditional surrender. And since God's terms were unacceptable to Pharaoh, he still refused to let the people of Israel go (Ex. 8:25-32).

Death of the Cattle

The fifth plague was against the domestic animals of the land (Ex. 9:1-7). These died, as the Lord had said. Only the cattle of the Israelites were spared.

We must judge this plague also by the particular religious veneration paid to animals in Egypt. One of the most popular of the religious cults was the cult of Apis, the bull god. At Memphis and at other shrines a sacred bull was kept within the temple and worshiped there by devotees. At one period of Egyptian history, dead bulls were given elaborate burials in vaults at Saqqara near Memphis. The Serapeum there contains niches for hundreds of these venerated animals.

The popularity of the worship of the bull can be seen in the fact that after the Exodus, when the Israelites thought that Moses had died on Mount Sinai, they gave their gold to be made into a calf in the image of Apis and cried out, "These are thy gods, O Israel, which brought thee up out of the land of Egypt" (Ex. 32:4).

Against this depraved religious system, God now brings a plague that means death to the cattle, presumably a contagious disease that spread like wildfire. All the cattle died, those in the fields and even those within the sacred enclosures of the Egyptian temples. Only the cattle of Israel were spared. Still Pharaoh hardened his heart.

Boils and Ulcers

The sixth plague seems to have followed quickly upon the plague that affected the livestock. But this one was worse. It was directed against the bodies of the people. We read, "And they took ashes of the furnace, and stood before Pharaoh; and Moses sprinkled it up toward heaven; and it became a boil breaking forth with ulcers upon man, and upon beast. And the magicians could not stand before Moses because of the boils, for the boil was upon the magicians, and upon all the Egyptians. And the Lord hardened the heart of Pharaoh, and he hearkened not unto them, as the Lord had spoken unto Moses" (Ex. 9:10-12).

How ironic this plague must have seemed to the Egyptians! It was the custom in Egypt for the ashes of the sacrifices to be sprinkled into the air above the worshipers. And all who had the ashes fall upon them counted it a blessing. Now, in the hands of Moses, the ashes of blessing became ashes of cursing. And even the priests who performed the sacrifices were so defiled that they could not enter the temple and stand before Moses.

But where were the gods of Egypt? In antiquity the land of Egypt was noted for its skill in medicine, and the gods of Egypt, who were always associated with medical practice, were known as gods of healing. Where was their healing power now? As the boils continued, the impotence of these gods was revealed to every Egyptian. But still Pharaoh refused to let the people go. Now there was to be no pause in the terrible judgments that followed.

Judgments Against the Sky

The first two plagues had been upon the Nile. The third, fourth, fifth, and sixth plagues were against the land. Now the sky was to be judged with the plagues of hail, locusts, and great darkness.

The seventh plague was an extraordinary phenomenon. It does not hail in Egypt and there is almost no rain. In fact there are years when the country knows nothing but sunshine. Now the skies were filled with clouds, and the Lord sent hail and fire, and lightning that ran along the ground. The Bible says, "So there was hail, and fire mingled with the hail, very grievous, such as there was none like it in all the land of Egypt since it became a nation. And the hail smote throughout all the land of Egypt all that were in the field, both man and beast; and the hail smote every herb of the field, and broke every tree of the field. Only in the land of Goshen, where the children of Israel were, was there no hail" (Ex. 9:24-26).

With this great destruction came the first turning in public opinion, a turning that would reach the palace of the Pharaoh with the next plague (Ex. 10:7). Moses had warned the people that every animal left in the fields would die, but that every animal brought under the cover of a barn or a house would be spared. Some of the people believed. We read, "He that feared the word of the Lord among the servants of Pharaoh made his servants and his cattle flee into the houses; and he that regarded not the word of the Lord left his servants and his cattle in the field" (Ex. 9:20, 21). For those who fled from the fields, faith in the sky gods was broken. Shu, the god of the atmosphere, Horus and Month, the bird gods, and Nut, the sky goddess, were ineffective against Jehovah, the God of Israel.

The eighth plague was a terrifying invasion of locusts that devoured all that had been left in the fields after the destruction by the hail. Before this plague the nobles at court had pleaded with the king to let the Hebrews go: "How long shall this man be a snare unto us? Let the men go, that they may serve the Lord their God. Knowest thou not yet that Egypt is destroyed?" (Ex. 10:7).

Pharaoh attempted to bargain with Moses. But God does not bargain. Moses left the palace. The night wind brought the locusts. All remaining vegetation was consumed. Nepri, the grain god, Anubis, the guardian of the fields, and Min, the deity of harvests and crops, took their places along with the other impotent and defeated gods of Egypt.

Eclipse of Ra

The ninth plague came swiftly and unannounced. It was the most significant of all in terms of the Egyptian religion. For three days a dense darkness fell upon the land, a darkness so intense that it could be felt. The stars were gone. The moon did not shine. And most terrible of all, Ra, the sun god, had been obliterated from his preeminent place in the heavens (Ex. 10:21-23).

One commentator, Donald Grey Barnhouse, describes the ninth plague in particularly vivid terms. Egypt, he says, "was the land of perpetual sunshine. Three hundred and sixty-five days in the year, the sun shines in Egypt. And three hundred and sixty-five nights in the year, the skies are so alight with moon and stars that there is little like it to be seen from earth. . . . Suddenly the sky and the light were eclipsed by a phenomenon that fell upon the land. . . . Life came to a halt. The people were forced to remain in their beds for three days. They were without food; they could not see each other; they lived, choking and gasping, in their beds." *(The Invisible War,* Donald Grey Barnhouse, Zondervan, Grand Rapids, Mich.)

The final judgment upon the sky and the sky gods was complete. The Pharaoh, as a sun worshiper, had discovered that the sun could not help him and that there was a greater power, Jehovah, who, in fact, had once called even the sun into existence.

Still the king of Egypt would not let the people of Israel go. With his heart hardened, the Pharaoh drove Moses from him saying, "Get thee from me, take heed to thyself, see my face no more; for in that day thou seest my face thou shalt die." Moses answered him, "Thou hast spoken well; I will see thy face again no more" (Ex. 10:28-29).

Jehovah, Our God

What are the spiritual lessons of the plagues? First, that of all the gods of this world, both demonic and imaginary, none deserves to be worshiped. Only one God, Jehovah, the God of Israel is the true God, and He alone is all-powerful.

Second, the inevitable result of any conflict with God is always disastrous to God's adversary. Consequently, it is utter folly for anyone at any time to resist or turn his back upon God.

Third, those who have been called by God and who stand with Him can be assured of His victory, even though it may be delayed and even though it may take great courage to stand with Him. If you are so called, then you may stand with Him courageously. And you may rejoice in the strength of Him who has permitted us to share in His victories.

CHAPTER SEVEN

THE DEATH OF THE LAMB

(EXODUS 11–12)

The final judgment of Jehovah upon the land of Egypt in Moses' day was the decisive one. It was also climactic, for with each of the earlier plagues the judgments had increased in intensity, and this one—the death of the firstborn—was cataclysmic.

In one sense the situation was parallel to the battles between the United States and Japan in World War II. After Japan's initial wave of conquest, the two countries engaged mostly in naval battles. After that there were the repeated air attacks in which the U.S. forces gained command of the air. Then there was the long series of U.S. assaults on the islands of the Pacific—Guadalcanal, Saipan, Iwo Jima, Okinawa, and others—in which the United States drew closer and closer to Japan itself and increasingly destroyed the power of the Japanese war machine. The final and climactic blow came with the unleashing of atomic bombs against the mainland of Japan. With that the war was over.

In the same way, the plagues upon Egypt began as plagues against the river, increased in intensity with various judgments against the land and sky, and culminated in a cataclysmic judgment against all the firstborn persons and animals of the country. In that judgment all the firstborn died, from the firstborn of the livestock to the firstborn of all classes of people in the nation (Ex. 12:29-30). In the aftermath of this judgment, Israel was at last set free.

Death of the Firstborn

We have already seen that each of the judgments had spiritual overtones, for each was directed against one or more of the gods of Egypt. This is also true of the last judgment. But this time the god was not Osiris or Nu (the Nile gods), or Geb (the god of the land). It was not Ra (the sun god) or Hathor, or Apis, or Hekt, or Horus, or Amon, or any of the thousands of other gods of the Egyptian pantheon. It was the Pharaoh himself, the incarnation of the sun god. Thus, when the firstborn in the house of the Pharaoh died, the next god died. The victory of Jehovah was complete, and obvious to all.

At the same time that this final judgment was taking place, however, God was establishing an observance in Israel which was to be a token of blessing and which was to continue throughout Israel's history. In fact, it continues to this day. It was the Passover. It is so important, not only for Israel but also for the Christian church, that we dare not treat it lightly. Here is the biblical account:

And the Lord spoke unto Moses and Aaron in the land of Egypt, saying, "This month shall be unto you the beginning of months; it shall be the first month of the year to you. Speak ye unto all the congregation of Israel, saying, [that] in the tenth day of this month they shall take to them every man a lamb, according to the house of their fathers, a lamb for an house; and if the household be too little for the lamb, let him and his neighbor next unto his house take it according to the number of the souls; every man according to his eating shall make your count for the lamb.

Your lamb shall be without blemish, a male of the first year; ye shall take it out from the sheep, or from the goats. And ye shall keep it until the fourteenth day of the same month, and the whole assembly of the congregation of Israel shall kill it in the evening. And they shall take of the blood, and strike it on the two side posts and on the upper doorpost of the houses, wherein they shall eat it. And they shall eat the flesh in that night, roasted with fire and unleavened bread; and with bitter herbs they shall eat it.

And thus shall ye eat it: with your loins girded, your shoes on your feet, and your staff in your hand; and ye shall eat it in haste: it is the Lord's passover. For I will pass through the land of Egypt this night, and will smite all the firstborn in the land of Egypt, both man and beast; and against all the gods of Egypt I will execute judgment: I am the Lord. And the blood shall be to you for a token upon the houses where ye are; and when I see the blood, I will pass over you, and the plague shall not be upon you to destroy you, when I smite the land of Egypt" (Ex. 12:1-8, 11-13).

We can understand these words better if we picture in our minds what they must have meant for the people. In the tenth day of the month of Nisan, which is approximately our month of April, the father of each Jewish family was to go to his fields or his barn and carefully pick a lamb for the Passover. The animal was to be without any spots or blemishes. When it was found, it was to be brought into the house and remain there until the fourteenth day of Nisan. From this point on, the entire family would be in on the ritual; the children would see the lamb, play with it, and then come to love it as any child would love a woolly little bundle of life.

THE DEATH OF THE LAMB

On the fourteenth day of Nisan, however, the lamb would be killed. The blood would be spread upon the two side posts and lintel of the door. The family would eat the lamb together. And to the shocked questions of the children who had just witnessed the killing of the innocent lamb, the father would reply that this was a sign to the Lord for Him to pass over the Hebrew household on the night when He passed through Egypt.

It would all have been very solemn as the family sat down to dinner that night, fully clothed and ready for their departure. At first there would have been silence except for the quiet small talk that went with the distribution of the lamb and bitter herbs. Then there would have been total silence in the home as the terrible plague began and the first wails of the mourners began to be heard in the city.

We must remember that Egypt is a country where people greet death as a great calamity and where mourning is intense and quite open. There would have been screams and crying. And all the while the Hebrew family would be sitting in silence, trembling a little, waiting for the moment that would signal their departure. Henceforth, the same mood would be recreated year by year as the family observed the event and remembered their deliverance.

What Israel Learned

It is evident that God delivered the people in this way in order to teach certain lessons about their past and future relationship to Him. And so, this study is not complete until we have discussed these lessons. What were the lessons that God taught the people of Israel through the Passover? What are the lessons He intends to teach us? The first and most obvious lesson is that Israel was also guilty before God, just as the Egyptians were guilty. This is proved by the fact that

Israel was only saved from the same plague by means of the sacrifice provided.

There were many reasons for the Hebrew people to think they were acceptable to God. For one thing, the fourth through the ninth plagues had occurred in such a way that the land in which the Israelites were living was spared. This might have encouraged them to think that they were intrinsically more holy than the Egyptians or more worthy of God's favor. But, of course, this was not the purpose of the distinction at all. It was merely to reveal God's power and sovereignty.

The people might have remembered their ancestry, and reasoned that because Abraham was a friend of God and because they traced their ancestry to him they had a privileged position and were spared on this basis. But this also was wrong thinking.

Somewhere in Egypt on that night was a young man named Joshua, one of the very few of that generation who lived to enter the Promised Land. When he had lived through a lifetime with God and with the people and was about to die, he faced this question firmly. He gathered the people around him and spoke to them, reminding them, not of their dazzling past, but of their ignoble ancestry. He said, "Your fathers dwelt on the other side of the river of old, even Terah, the father of Abraham, and the father of Nahor; and they served other gods. . . . Now, therefore, fear the Lord, and serve Him in sincerity and in truth; and put away the gods which your fathers served on the other side of the river, and in Egypt, and serve ye the Lord" (Josh. 24:2, 14).

Others would have thought that they were deserving of special treatment because they had received God's revelation of Himself, not only through Abraham, but through the other patriarchs and through Moses. They did not worship the demon gods of Egypt, they would say. They worshiped

Jehovah and did so because of His revelation to them. But the truth of the situation was that they did worship the demon gods of Egypt. And what is more, they continued to do so even after their deliverance, as their subsequent history shows.

Well, then, we ask, why did God treat them differently and deliver them from slavery? Why? Because of His grace. *Sola gratia!* There was no other reason. In themselves the people of Israel deserved God's judgment as much as the Egyptians. In fact, they would have experienced that judgment—even to the loss of every firstborn child in Israel—had God not established the sacrifice by which the doorposts were marked and death diverted. And they all knew it. They learned, as Moses later wrote for them, that "the Lord did not set His love upon you, nor choose you, because ye were more in number than any people, for ye were the fewest of all people. But because the Lord loved you, and because He would keep the oath which He had sworn unto your fathers, hath the Lord . . . redeemed you" (Deut. 7:7-8). They deserved to die, but God saved them. He saved them by grace. And, of course, it is only by grace that God saves His people today.

Through Faith

The first great truth that the Passover was designed to teach was that Israel also deserved God's judgment and was saved by grace alone. But there was another truth to be taught. It was that even though salvation is entirely by grace, it nevertheless comes to man through the channel of a human response or, as we say, through faith.

It was not enough for a firstborn Hebrew on the night of the Passover in Egypt to be a Hebrew, His being a Hebrew would not have saved him. It was not enough for him to have heard the instructions for the Passover given to the people through Moses or even to have believed them intellectually. The hearing or the believing would not have saved him. If he were to be saved, he must do what God required. And this meant that he must remain with his family in the house upon which the blood had been spread. Thus, he must give evidence of his belief by acting unequivocally upon it.

In the same way God comes to you. He does not look to your ancestry, social status, or intellectual achievements. He does ask you to believe Him and to act upon your belief. He tells you that you are condemned because of sin in your life (Rom. 3:23; 6:23). And He adds that He has provided a sacrifice, a substitute, for you in the person of His Son, our Lord Jesus Christ (Rom. 5:6-8). He asks that you believe that. He asks that you turn from all attempts to earn His approval and receive the salvation that He provides freely. If you will do that, then the angel of eternal death will pass over you. And you will take your place as one of God's children forever.

Death of the Lamb

The final truth that the Passover was meant to impress upon the minds of the people was that in order for there to be salvation, there had to be the killing of the lamb. There must be death. Blood must be shed. For, as the Bible says, "Without shedding of blood [there] is no remission [of sins]" (Heb. 9:22; cf. Lev. 17:11).

Many people do not like this doctrine. They think it is barbaric or out of place in our supposedly more genteel day. But we must not think that the idea was any more palatable years ago in Israel. We can be sure that the blood spread upon the doorposts was distasteful to many of the Hebrews of Moses' day. And the killing of the lamb would have been a difficult thing in a household, particularly where children had become attached to it. They would have protested its death, and the parents would have killed it reluctantly. However, if the lamb had not died, the oldest child would have.

By the sacrifice, God taught that there must be death to atone for sin—the wages of sin is death—either the death of the offender or the death of the innocent substitute. God thereby prepared the way for people to understand the death of the Lord Jesus Christ when He came.

The Lamb of God

New Testament writers often refer to the sacrifice of lambs in Israel in explaining the death of the Lord Jesus Christ. The Apostle Paul writes, "For even Christ, our passover, is sacrificed for us" (1 Cor. 5:7). Peter says, "Forasmuch as ye know that ye were not redeemed with corruptible things, like silver and gold, from your vain manner of life received by tradition from your fathers, but with the precious blood of Christ, as of a lamb without blemish and without spot" (1 Peter 1:18-19). John the Baptist cried, "Behold the Lamb of God, who taketh away the sin of the world" (John 1:29). These references are not accidental. Nor are they merely examples of vivid Hebrew imagery.

Why is the death of the Lord Jesus Christ described in this way? Because God Himself took this means to explain it. In some ways it was a lesson that God had been teaching throughout all the years of man's history. In the Garden of Eden, God had killed an animal in order to clothe our first sinful parents (Gen. 3:21). That was a one-to-one relationship—one lamb for one person. On the night of the Passover, one lamb was killed for each family—one lamb for several persons (Ex. 12:3-4). Later, at Sinai, when the Law was given to the newly emerged nation, God taught that on the

Day of Atonement one lamb should be killed for the nation (Lev. 16:15-16). Then, years later when Jesus Christ was about to begin His public ministry, John the Baptist came crying, "Behold the Lamb of God, who taketh away the sin of the world" (John 1:29). One lamb for one person, one lamb for one family, one lamb for one nation, one Lamb for all humanity. He is the one Lamb for our sin, however great or heinous it may be.

Where is your sin? How is it to be judged? It can only be in one of two places. It can be on you. In that case you must bear its judgment, and you are today in the same position as a firstborn Egyptian or a firstborn Israelite apart from the sacrifice that God has provided. Or—and this is the glorious possibility—it can be on Jesus Christ. In that case He has already borne its judgment. He has paid its penalty. His blood was shed. He has become your Passover. If your faith is in Christ, then the angel of death has already passed over you, and there is nothing left for you but heaven.

CHAPTER EIGHT

THE CLOUD IN THE DESERT

(EXODUS 13:21-22)

In the opening pages of Russell H. Conwell's inspirational classic, *Acres of Diamonds*, the well-known preacher and educator tells a story he learned from an old Arab guide in Persia. It is the story of a rich man named Ali Hafed, who was content with his riches until he learned about diamonds. He had never thought about diamonds before—he did not even know about them. But now he began to aspire to the kind of wealth they would bring. Eventually, he left home in pursuit of them. Over a period of years, Hafed used up his money in searching and at last died a poor man on the shores of the Bay of Barcelona. Meanwhile, back in Persia, the man who had purchased Hafed's farm found an unusual pebble in the brook where the former owner had often watered his cattle. It turned out to be a diamond. Soon more were discovered. In this way, said Conwell's guide, the world-famous Golconda mines developed, from which have been taken many of the most famous jewels of the crowned heads of Europe.

Arab stories always seem to have morals, and the moral of

this story is that Ali Hafed went hunting for wealth when actually he had acres of diamonds in the front yard of his own home. My moral, which is a slightly different one, is that this is often true spiritually—in a study of the Word of God.

The subject to which we now come can be a field of diamonds to the one taking the time to discover it. And yet—this strikes me as surprising—few studies have been made of the topic. I refer to the great cloud that led and protected the Israelites during their 40 years of wandering in the wilderness prior to their conquest of Canaan. Its neglect is surprising, first, in the light of its unique and striking nature, and second, because of the frequency with which it is mentioned in both the Old and New Testaments. The cloud is mentioned 58 times in the Bible—more frequently than the names of Bethlehem or Nazareth, for instance, and more often than the names of persons such as Cain and Abel, Mary and Joseph, Herod, Isaiah, or Satan.

The cloud is first mentioned at the time of the Exodus when it appeared to protect the people from the pursuing Egyptians and to guide them in their journeys. The Bible says, "And the Lord went before them by day in a pillar of a cloud, to lead them the way; and by night in a pillar of fire, to give them light; to go by day and night: He took not away the pillar of the cloud by day, nor the pillar of fire by night, from before the people" (Ex. 13:21-22).

After this the cloud is spoken of many other times throughout the Pentateuch (Genesis through Deuteronomy). Years later it appears at the dedication of Solomon's temple (1 Kings 8:10). It is entirely possible that the same phenomenon is referred to on several later occasions, including the transfiguration and ascension of Jesus Christ. The cloud is of great significance, and the passages that mention it teach great spiritual lessons.

THE CLOUD IN THE DESERT

A Unique Phenomenon

It is important to recognize at the start that the cloud in the desert was unlike any other cloud that the world had ever seen. It was called a cloud only because the Hebrew language of the time had no other word to describe it.

We have an analogy in the way we chose to describe the appearance of the first atomic bomb blasts. Here was a phenomenon that no one on earth had seen before. Because of its shape, the phenomenon was called a mushroom cloud. Of course, it was not a cloud at all. And it was a mushroom only in the sense that it appeared to have a stem and a large rounded top. No one either then or now has taken the words literally.

The infant Hebrew nation had a similar experience. Shortly after their departure from Goshen in the land of Egypt, while on the way to the Red Sea, this unique thing appeared. It was large, as we shall see later, and it possessed unusual properties. It appeared as a cloud in the daytime but, during the night, it gave off light and warmth so that it seemed to be a pillar of fire.

Generally the cloud or pillar of fire was located in the center of the camp of the Israelites. But during the first days of Israel's march from Egypt, it moved behind the people so that it provided protection against the pursuing Egyptians (Ex. 14:19-20). Later during their march, it went before them to lead the way (Ex. 40:36-38).

On the night of the Red Sea crossing, this cloud or pillar that stood behind the Israelite camp gave off light toward them but showed darkness toward the Egyptians. Thus the possibility of night raids or a sudden attack was excluded.

What were the people to call this unprecedented phenomenon? There were no words to describe it. Consequently sometimes they called it "the glory" or "the radiance" (meaning the glory or the radiance of God); most often it was called simply "the cloud." In the Old Testament the term "the cloud" almost always points to this phenomenon.

God's Protection

The second thing we need to recognize is that without the cloud and without the miracle that it represented, the people of Israel would have perished in the desert many years before they actually entered Canaan. The cloud protected them, first, from human enemies like Pharaoh and the Egyptian armies, and second, from the natural dangers of the desert.

We must remember at this point that the number of people who left Egypt with Moses was extremely large and that they were going out into an area of the world that was—and still is—one of the most inhospitable on earth. The Bible tells us that 600,000 men belonged to the nation at the time of the Exodus (Ex. 12:37). In addition, there were wives and children. And the people of Israel were accompanied by a mixed multitude of former slaves from other nations who had left Egypt with them. The whole number must have been in excess of two million people.

Most of us have no way of appreciating how large a group of persons this was, for we have never seen so many, and a million of anything is almost beyond our comprehension. We can gain some idea of the size of this great mass of people, however, by remembering that the giant stadium in Pasadena, California, where the Rose Bowl classic is held each New Year's Day, when filled to capacity, holds about 104,000 people. If we imagine a crowd that size, and then multiply it 20 times, we will have an idea of the number of the Israelites and those who went with them.

These people, under the direction of Moses, were going out into the desert, where the temperature goes above 100° in the daytime and often falls to below freezing at night. A friend and I visited Egypt one July and were much amused by the description of the temperature of Egypt by those who lived there. When we landed at Alexandria in the extreme north of Egypt on the Mediterranean, we thought it was hot. It was undoubtedly over 100 degrees. But the people who lived in Alexandria said, "Oh, it's not so hot here in Alexandria. Alexandria is on the sea, and the temperatures here are moderate. Wait until you get to Cairo. There it *is* hot, and there are many flies."

We went on to Cairo, and they were right. It was hotter in Cairo. But there the people said, "Oh, it is not too bad here; we are still in the north of Egypt, in the delta region. Wait until you get to Luxor. There it is very hot, and there are flies."

After about a week in Cairo, we went on to Luxor, and in Luxor they were saying, "It is not really too hot here; the place where it is really hot is Aswan."

Our travels stopped at Luxor. We never got to Aswan. But even at Luxor, we were several hundred miles up the Nile from Alexandria, on the verge of the desert. The temperature rose to 140° in the sun in the daytime and fell close to 30° at night. We learned that the desert is most inhospitable and that we or anyone else would quickly die there, were it not for three things: proper guidance, shade from the sun, and water.

It was into such a land that the Lord was leading the two million former slaves who had left Egypt with Moses. It is not difficult to see that they would have perished in the extremes of temperature in the desert, by night and by day, if it had not been for the great miracle of the cloud that God caused to go with them.

What did the cloud do? For one thing, it was large enough to spread out over the entire camp of the Israelites. During the day it served as a covering from the direct rays of the sun, and during the night—when it changed to a pillar of fire—it gave warmth from the chill of the desert.

This is why one of the psalms, written hundreds of years later, says, "Egypt was glad when they departed; for the fear of them fell upon them. He spread a cloud for a covering, and fire to give light in the night" (Ps. 105:38-39). It is also why we sing these words in one of our great 18th-century hymns:

Round each habitation hovering,
  See the cloud and fire appear.
For a glory and a covering,
  Showing that the Lord is near:
Thus, deriving from their banner
  Light by night and shade by day,
Safe they feed upon the manna
  Which He gives them when they pray.

Seen in this light, it is evident that the presence of the cloud was a reminder of God's care for His people and of His constant protection.

God's Presence

The cloud was not only a reminder of God's protection, it was also a symbol of God's presence. For God was with His people, and the cloud showed it. God spoke from the cloud. He spoke from the cloud on Sinai when He gave the Law to Moses (Ex. 19:16-19; 24:16). He spoke from the cloud when it was standing over the Ark of the Covenant in the Holy of Holies of the Hebrew wilderness tabernacle (Ex. 33:7-11). And it was from the cloud that God spoke in judgment against the various movements of rebellion during the years of wilderness wandering (Num. 12:5-10).

God's symbolic presence is demonstrated in this account of

the moving of the cloud: "And they departed from the mount of the Lord three days' journey; and the Ark of the Covenant of the Lord went before them in the three days' journey, to search out a resting place for them. And the cloud of the Lord was upon them by day, when they went out of the camp. And it came to pass, when the Ark set forward, that Moses said, Rise up, Lord, and let Thine enemies be scattered, and let them that hate Thee flee before Thee. And when it rested, he said, Return, O Lord, unto the many thousands of Israel" (Num. 10:33-36). At no time in their wandering were the people of Israel able to forget—even if they wanted to—that the presence of God went with them and overshadowed all that they did.

Do you realize that your life is under the constant scrutiny of God? You should, for it is as true for you as it was for them. And it should change your conduct. One of the great collects of the liturgical church acknowledges this truth quite clearly when it says, "Almighty God, unto whom all hearts are open, all desires known, and from whom no secrets are hid; cleanse the thoughts of our hearts by the inspiration of Thy Holy Spirit, that we may perfectly love Thee, and worthily magnify Thy holy Name. . . ." If we really acknowledged to ourselves the truth of that statement—that our hearts and our actions are open before Him—how changed some of our conduct would be!

God's Leading

The cloud was a tool for the care and protection of the people. It was a symbol of God's presence. But it was also a very practical means by which God led them in the wilderness and thereby trained them in absolute obedience.

This function of the cloud is described clearly in two passages, one at the very end of Exodus and the other in the ninth chapter of Numbers. The Numbers passage, which is the more complete and graphic of the two, reads:

On the day that the tabernacle was reared up the cloud covered the tabernacle, namely, the tent of the testimony; and at evening there was upon the tabernacle, as it were, the appearance of fire, until the morning. So it was always: the cloud covered it by day, and the appearance of fire by night.

And when the cloud was taken up from the tabernacle, then after that the Children of Israel journeyed; and in the place where the cloud abode, there the Children of Israel pitched their tents. At the commandment of the Lord the Children of Israel journeyed, and at the commandment of the Lord they encamped; as long as the cloud abode upon the tabernacle they rested in their tents.

And when the cloud tarried long upon the tabernacle many days, then the Children of Israel kept the charge of the Lord, and journeyed not. And so it was, when the cloud was a few days upon the tabernacle, according to the commandment of the Lord they abode in their tents, and according to the commandment of the Lord they journeyed. And so it was, when the cloud abode from evening unto the morning, and that the cloud was taken up in the morning, then they journeyed; whether it was by day or by night that the cloud was taken up, they journeyed. Or whether it were two days, or a month, or a year, that the cloud tarried upon the tabernacle, remaining thereon, the Children of Israel abode in their tents, and journeyed not; but when it was taken up, they journeyed. At the commandment of the Lord they rested in the tents, and at the commandment of the Lord they journeyed: they kept the charge of the Lord, at the commandment of the Lord by the hand of Moses" (Num. 9:15-23).

THE CLOUD IN THE DESERT

We must exercise our imaginations here in order to visualize how it must have been in the camp when the cloud of the Lord stopped or moved forward. We often tend to imagine past spiritual events as being better than they actually were, in this case by picturing the people joyfully moving forward under the protecting cloud. But there is no evidence to suggest that they were joyful. In fact, the opposite is far more likely to have been true.

We must picture a family of Hebrews coming to rest in the middle of a long afternoon, after a four- or five-hour march during which the cloud has been moving on before them. It has now stopped. And that is the signal for the family to stop and begin unpacking. The tents are put up, the bedding unrolled, the cooking utensils brought out and arranged, and the animals unharnessed.

Dinner is prepared and served, and the family is just about to lie down for the night when suddenly someone calls out over the camp, "The cloud is moving!" The family looks up. Sure enough, the cloud is moving. So, reluctantly, they strike camp, pack the baggage, and begin to follow it.

One hour later the cloud stops again. They look at each other and say, "Well, He's not going to catch us this time. We'll just leave the baggage packed and sleep on the ground."

Morning comes, and the cloud is still there. It is still there at evening, and on the next evening and the next. A week goes by, two weeks, three. Finally the father says, "Well, I suppose we had better get it over with." So they unpack.

They no sooner get the tent erected and the cooking utensils laid out than someone shouts again, "The cloud is moving!" And they have to start packing and get on the move.

Did the people of Israel rejoice in the way God led them? They did not! They hated the leading. If they could have done so, they would have lynched Moses and elected his brother Aaron, or some other weak person, to take them back to Egypt.

Like it or not, the people had to follow the cloud. If someone had said, "I don't care if the cloud is moving; I'm going to stay right here," he might have stayed, but he would soon have been alone in the heat of the desert. And he would have died there, either from the heat of the day or from the freezing temperatures at night.

No, the people hated the cloud. They hated its moving. But through this discipline—no matter how distasteful it was or how despised it became—God in His great wisdom was molding a nation of rabble into a force that would one day conquer Canaan.

In the same way, it is often through a rigorous and sometimes distasteful course of discipline that God molds us into an army of Christian warriors today.

The Holy Spirit

Someone will say, "Oh, that is an unfair comparison. They had the cloud, but we have nothing similar by which God can lead us or protect us today."

Oh? Are you sure that is right? They had the cloud; that is true. But what do we have? We have the Holy Spirit, the very life of God Almighty within, and the Holy Spirit is to us in every respect what the cloud was to them.

Was the cloud a symbol of God's presence? So is the Holy Spirit. In fact, He is actually God present. Did the cloud protect and lead the people? So does the Holy Spirit protect and lead us. That is why Jesus Christ could say in His final instruction to His disciples before His crucifixion, "When He, the Spirit of truth, is come, He will guide you into all truth" (John 16:13), and, "When He is come, He will reprove the world of sin, and of righteousness, and of judgment"

(John 16:8). And Paul can add, "Walk in the Spirit, and ye shall not fulfill the lust of the flesh" (Gal. 5:16).

If you are a Christian and are willing to obey God, the Holy Spirit will lead you. And what is more, He will lead you personally. He will train you to be an effective Christian soldier.

MOSES' FINEST HOUR

(EXODUS 32)

Spring 1940. France had fallen to the onrushing columns of the German war machine. The 350,000-man British army in France had made a harrowing evacuation from Dunkirk. Winston Churchill rose to speak before the House of Commons, and among other things, to introduce a new and striking phrase to the English language.

Churchill said, "Let us therefore brace ourselves to our duty and so bear ourselves that if the British Commonwealth and Empire last for a thousand years, men will still say, 'This was *their finest hour.*' "

It was a great expression. For it recognized that moments of crises provide the stepping stones for all men and women either to grandeur or to dismal failure.

In this study we shall be looking at an early incident in Israel's history that was the occasion for the finest hour in the life of Moses.

What was his finest hour? Was it when he stood before Pharaoh with God's command on his lips: "Let My people go"? No, that was not his finest hour.

MOSES' FINEST HOUR

Was it the moment in which he first looked from Mount Nebo upon the land to which he had brought the Hebrew nation? No, that was rewarding, but it was not his finest hour.

Was it the hour in which he turned his back on the Egyptian court, "choosing rather to suffer affliction with the people of God than to enjoy the pleasures of sin for a season?" (Heb. 11:25) No.

Moses' finest hour is recorded for us in Exodus 32, a chapter which tells of a great rebellion and apostasy on the part of the Hebrew people, and of the fact that Moses actually asked God to send him to hell if only He would spare them from destruction.

Sin in the Camp

Under the direction of Moses, the people had come from Egypt to Mount Sinai where God was to give them the Law. Moses was called up into the mountain to receive it. The Bible says that God descended upon the mountain in the midst of a cloud of smoke and fire. The sight was so awe-inspiring that the people were frightened, and even Moses said, "I exceedingly fear and quake" (Heb. 12:21). Nevertheless, Moses spent 40 days upon the mountain receiving the Ten Commandments and much of the Old Testament Law.

As the hours turned to days and the days to weeks, the people who were left in the valley gradually overcame their awe of the cloud on the mountain and grew cynical and impatient. They said, in effect, "Where is this man Moses, the man who brought us up out of the land of Egypt? We do not know what has become of him."

Before long they began to remember the worship of Apis the bull and Hathor the cow that they had known in Egypt. They asked Aaron, the brother of Moses, to make an image of Apis or Hathor for them.

Aaron should have refused, but he was weak, like many Christians. So he took their gold, melted it in the fire, and when he was done he had enough of the metal to make a little calf. That satisfied the people. They began to sing and dance and to worship the calf saying, "These are thy gods, O Israel, which brought thee up out of the land of Egypt" (Ex. 32:4).

It was not long before this debased and degenerate worship gave place to other debased and degenerate actions, as the worship of anything but the true and holy God always does. The people began to take off their clothes and throw themselves into an orgy.

Meanwhile, up on the mountain, God was still speaking to Moses. But God knew what was going on in the valley, and He angrily interrupted the giving of the Law to send Moses back down to the people.

How ironic the situation was! And how horrible! God had just given Moses the Ten Commandments. But while God was giving the Ten Commandments, the people of Israel were already breaking them.

The commandments instruct, "I am the Lord thy God, who have brought thee out of the land of Egypt, out of the house of bondage. Thou shalt have no other gods before Me. Thou shalt not make unto thee any carved image, or any likeness of anything that is in heaven above, or that is in the earth beneath, or that is in the water under the earth; thou shalt not bow down thyself to them, nor serve them; for I, the Lord thy God, am a jealous God, visiting the iniquity of the fathers upon the children unto the third and fourth generation of them that hate me" (Ex. 20:2-5). The very practice God forbade, the making and worshiping of images, was going full tilt among the people even while God was communicating the commandment against it to Moses.

There is another bit of irony in the story. While the debauchery was going on in the valley, upon the mountain God and Moses exchanged words in a way that would be genuinely funny if it were not so horrible. The Lord said to Moses, "Go, get thee down, for thy people, whom thou broughtest out of the land of Egypt, have corrupted themselves" (Ex. 32:7). After He had gone on to describe to a shocked Moses what was happening, Moses answered, "Lord, why doth Thy wrath burn against Thy people, whom Thou hast brought forth out of the land of Egypt with great power, and with a mighty hand?" (Ex. 32:11.)

"They are *your* people and *you* delivered them," God said to Moses.

"They are *Your* people," said Moses. "And *You* are the one who brought them up out of Egypt."

It was exactly the same situation that exists between a father and mother when their child begins to act abominably. The father says to the mother, "Well, don't you think you had better do something about *your* son?"

And his wife says, "What do you mean, '*my* son'? What are you going to do about *your* son?"

Neither wants to claim him in his present state. In the same way neither Moses nor the Lord seemed to want to acknowledge the people in their depraved and sinful condition.

An Act of Love

The lesson at this point is that in spite of God's grace, sin must always be dealt with, even at the human level. So Moses began to deal with it in the best way he knew. In anger he had smashed the stone tables of the Law that God had given him. Now in righteous anger he enters the camp, rebukes Aaron publicly, and calls for all who remain on the

Lord's side to come forth and stand beside him. The tribe of Levi responds. At Moses' command, the Levites are sent among the people with drawn swords to slay those who led the rebellion. The Bible tells us that of the two million people who had come out of the land of Egypt, 3,000 persons, or slightly over one-tenth of one per cent were slain. The golden calf was destroyed. Then, Moses called on the rest to reconsecrate themselves and their families to God.

We must look carefully at the situation at this point. From a human point of view, Moses had dealt with the sin. The leaders were punished, and the loyalty of the people was at least temporarily reclaimed. All seemed to be well. But Moses not only stood in a special relationship to the people, he also stood in a special relationship to God. And God still waited in wrath upon the mountain.

By this time not all of the Law had been given, but Moses had received enough of it to know something of the horror of sin and the uncompromising righteousness of God. Had not God said, "Thou shalt have no other gods before Me"? Had He not promised to visit the iniquity of the fathers upon the children even unto the third and fourth generations? How could Moses think that the limited judgment he had begun would satisfy the holiness of this great God?

Up on the mountain, Moses had said that the people were God's people. But now he knew that they were his people also, and he knew that he loved them.

The night passed, and the morning came. Moses was once again to ascend the mountain. During the sleepless night, Moses had come upon an idea—an idea that might possibly divert the just wrath of God. He had remembered the sacrifices of the Hebrew patriarchs and the newly instituted sacrifice of the Passover. Certainly, God had shown by these sacrifices that He was prepared to accept the death of an innocent substitute in place of the just death of the sinner.

Perhaps God would accept. . . . At this point Moses would hardly have voiced his idea. But when morning came, with great determination in his heart he began to ascend the mountain. In an agony of love he now prepared to make the most selfless offer that had ever been made by man.

Moses reached the top of the mountain and began to speak to God. It must have been in great anguish, for the Hebrew text is uneven and the second sentence which Moses speaks breaks off without ending. The fact is indicated by the presence of a dash and a semicolon in the middle of the King James translation of Exodus 32:32.

Moses' prayer was a strangled cry, a gasping sob, welling up from the heart of a man who was asking to be sent to hell if only it could mean the salvation of the people he had come to love. The Bible says, "And Moses returned unto the Lord, and said, Oh, this people have sinned a great sin, and have made them gods of gold. Yet now, if Thou wilt forgive their sin—;and if not, blot me, I pray thee, out of Thy book which Thou hast written" (Ex. 32:31-32). At this point there is a sublime irony among all the sad ironies of the story, an exchange between God and Moses that is wonderful enough to make men weep.

On the preceding day, moments before Moses had come down from the mountain, God had said something that would have been a great temptation to a lesser man. He had said that if Moses would agree, He would destroy the people for their sin and would begin to make a new Hebrew nation from Moses. The exact words are, "Now therefore let Me alone, that My wrath may burn against them, and that I may consume them, and I will make of thee a great nation" (Ex. 32:10). Moses had rejected the offer.

After Moses had been with the people, his answer, again a negative, rose to even finer heights. God had said, "I will destroy them and make a great nation of you." Moses said that God should rather destroy him and save the nation. Oh, the love of this man Moses! He had seen the sin of Israel. Already they had rebelled against him and turned their backs on his leadership. They would do so again. They would forever rebel against God. But still Moses loved them. He wished to spare them. Thus, he cries, "Blot me, I pray Thee, out of Thy Book."

Paul's Offer

This offer of Moses, so simply told in this great chapter of Exodus, is approached by only one other man mentioned in the Bible. The man is Paul. But Paul knew in a way that Moses could not know that the request he made was impossible. And hence his statement, while equally full of feeling, is free of Moses' struggle.

Paul's statement occurs in Romans 9, at the beginning of a section in which Paul is to discuss the present unbelief and future destiny of the Hebrews. Now we must remember as we read this that Paul was a Jew by birth and education and that he was proud of his heritage. What is more, he agonized over the unbelief of the people to whom Christ first came and to whom the Gospel had been so long and so earnestly preached. Nothing in all of Paul's experience indicated that there would be a mass turning to the Messiah by the Jews, and hence, along with his agony for them, he feared some temporal act of God's judgment upon them.

Moreover, as an astute observer of events in Judea and in the Roman world, Paul must have observed the rising tide of nationalism spurred on by the Zealots, and feared that it was soon to engulf the country and end in terrible destruction as it did in A.D. 70 under the armies of Titus. Paul must have worried about it more and more as time passed, for his letters contain increasingly clear warnings about obeying the secular powers and pursuing peace.

As a student of Christ's life, Paul must also have known of His prophecies concerning Jerusalem. Jesus had said, "And when ye shall see Jerusalem compassed with armies, then know that its desolation is near. . . . For these are the days of vengeance, that all things which are written may be fulfilled. . . . For there shall be great distress in the land, and wrath upon this people. And they shall fall by the edge of the sword, and shall be led away captive into all nations; and Jerusalem shall be trodden down by the Gentiles, until the times of the Gentiles be fulfilled" (Luke 21:20, 22-24).

In the light of these prophecies and the growing unrest around him, Paul must have feared for the Jewish people. Out of his great love for them, he wrote, "I say the truth in Christ, I lie not, my conscience also bearing me witness in the Holy Spirit, that I have great heaviness and continual sorrow in my heart. For I could wish that I myself were accursed from Christ for my brethren, my kinsmen according to the flesh" (Rom. 9:1-3).

Like Moses, Paul was saying that he would consent to be sent to hell if it could mean the salvation of the sinful, rebellious, unbelieving people whom he loved.

The Only Sacrifice

We must realize that what Paul prayed for and what Moses prayed for could not be. Neither Paul nor Moses could save even themselves, let alone a nation, from God's just wrath against sin, for they themselves were sinners. Moses was actually a murderer. And Paul had stood by consenting while others took the life of the deacon Stephen. Out of the love which God had caused to grow up within them, each offered to be the substitute. But neither could qualify. Neither could die for others.

But there was One who could. Thus, "when the fullness of the time was come, God sent forth His Son, made of a woman, made under the law, to redeem them that were under the law, that we might receive the adoption of sons" (Gal. 4:4-5).

People today are much like Israel of old. God is in His holy mountain. While He is there, we are in the valley of this world breaking His commandments and turning our backs on the very One who gave us life and sustains us on this earth.

Our sin makes us subject to God's wrath. But God, in His mercy, provides a remedy through Christ. As the Saviour faced the cross, He said to God, "I am willing to be sent to hell, to be separated from You, My Father, if only it can bring about the salvation of these sinful, rebellious, unbelieving people whom I love."

And God said, "This sacrifice I will accept. You will be cursed for others. My just wrath will fall on You rather than on them. You shall be cut off from My presence. Then, on the basis of Your sacrifice, I will deal mercifully with them. I will cleanse their sin. And I will make them a kingdom of priests unto Me forever."

Do you believe that? Will you commit yourself to Christ? If you do, God will spare you the just consequences of your sin. He will cleanse you of all unrighteousness. He will give you a new spirit formed by His love and capable even of sacrificing your own salvation for that of others—if it were necessary or possible.

PART THREE

David

The Greatest King

THE CHOICE
OF A KING

(1 SAMUEL 16:1-13; 1 SAMUEL 18; 2 SAMUEL 5:5)

One summer when I was visiting a small country of the Near East, I noticed a number of posters on which were emblazoned the head and name of a man whom I have since forgotten. I could hardly miss them, for they were everywhere. "Who is that man?" I asked somebody.

"Don't you know who that is?" he replied in shock, and then gave his name. "He is our hero. Everybody knows about him."

But I had not heard about him, and I have never heard about him since. It set me thinking how every country has its national heroes. Indeed, countries seem unable to survive without them.

The United States has George Washington and Abraham Lincoln. England has Henry IV, Sir Winston Churchill, and others. Switzerland has its William Tell. But it would take all those that I have mentioned plus others to equal the character and personal accomplishments of Israel's great leader and hero, King David. Moreover, he is important not just to Israel but to the whole world.

James Hastings has written in *The Greater Men and Women of the Bible:* "The David of Israel is not simply the greatest of her kings; he is the man great in everything. He monopolizes all her institutions. He is her shepherd boy—the representative of her toiling classes. He is her musician—the successor of Jubal and Miriam and Deborah. He is her soldier—the conqueror of the Goliaths that would steal her peace. He is her king—numbering her armies and regulating her polity. He is her priest—substituting a broken and a contrite spirit for the blood of bulls and rams. He is her prophet—presaging with his last breath the everlastingness of his kingdom. He is her poet—most of her psalms are called by his name."

The influence of David's greatness extended far beyond the ancient Jewish nation, however. Through the wise administration of his kingdom and through his victories, a large measure of peace came to the then turbulent Near East. With peace came prosperity. Monumental advances in commerce, trade, government, and the arts followed and, in some cases, continued for centuries. Trade expanded into Syria, Egypt, and Arabia. In many of these lands, ancient carvings and texts reveal a widespread knowledge of Hebrew commerce, music, and poetry.

David's own poetry has come down to us through his psalms. Many persons who do not know a word spoken by George Washington or Abraham Lincoln are steeped in these verses. Through many of the psalms, David emerges as a prophet of the coming Messiah; and Christians can never forget that it was through David's royal and legal line that Jesus, the Messiah, entered history nearly 2,000 years ago.

God's Choice

In view of all these accomplishments, it is somewhat of a surprise to turn to 1 Samuel 16, to the first mention of David in the Old Testament, and find that he appears not as a hero but as a youth who was for the most part overlooked by his family. This, of course, is a main point of the passage. For it is apparent, even in the most casual reading, that the author is emphasizing that the choice of David to be king was not man's choice but God's.

The Scripture tells us that the Prophet Samuel had been grieving over God's rejection of King Saul, David's predecessor. Apparently Samuel deeply loved the erring Saul. But God had come to him saying, "How long wilt thou mourn for Saul, seeing I have rejected him from reigning over Israel? Fill thine horn with oil, and go; I will send thee to Jesse, the Bethlehemite; for I have provided Me a king among his sons" (1 Sam. 16:1). In response to these directions, Samuel journeyed to Bethlehem where he prepared a sacrifice to which he invited Jesse and his sons.

The first son, Eliab, must have been a magnificent specimen. For when Samuel saw Eliab, Samuel followed the normal course of human thinking and said, "Surely the Lord's anointed is before Him" (v. 6). If the choice had been left to Samuel, godly though he was, he would undoubtedly have chosen Eliab, who would have been another Saul. But God said to the prophet, "Look not on his countenance, or on the height of his stature, because I have refused him; for the Lord seeth not as man seeth; for man looketh on the outward appearance, but the Lord looketh on the heart" (v. 7).

Next came Abinadab, the second son. And Samuel said, "Neither hath the Lord chosen this one" (v. 8). Shammah came, and Shammah was not chosen either. Neither were any of the other sons who were present. Finally, after the prophets careful questioning, David, the youngest, was summoned. When he came, fresh from keeping the sheep, the Lord said, "Arise, anoint him; for this is he" (v. 12). We then read that the Spirit of the Lord came on David from that day forward. This is the first great principle of any spiritual blessing. The choice must be God's. If the choice were left to you or me, we would choose Saul or Eliab. And we would choose wrongly. Only God can choose properly. Hence we shall experience spiritual blessing only in those actions and those deeds that originate with Him.

God's Vision

Some people question why God cannot bless actions that originate with man. But the answer is made perfectly clear in the story. It is because only God can see a situation correctly. God knows what is in the heart of man. God knows the end from the beginning.

The key is verse 7: "For the Lord seeth not as man seeth; for man looketh on the outward appearance, but the Lord looketh on the heart." These words are not only a statement of the clearness of God's vision and His capacity to judge, they are also a statement of our limitations. And, of course, this is the crux of the problem. It is not just that God can see clearly. It is that God *alone* can see clearly. At best we see only the outward appearances.

The choice of a person for any spiritual work must be God's. Not only are you and I unable to see a man's heart, there is also the fact that even if we could see it, we cannot assess it properly, due to sin. Like a bad camera lens, sin distorts and inverts our vision.

The Unexpected

There is an application here that we should not miss. If we really cannot see as God sees, and if we cannot assess the heart as God assesses it, then it must follow that when God chooses people for spiritual work the people themselves may come from what are to us the most unexpected places. We will not often find them among the great of the earth or those who commend themselves to us for their intellect, bearing, or outstanding qualities of leadership. When we look for capable leaders, we look up. God says, "When I look for a man who is to serve Me faithfully, I look low down" (see 1 Cor. 1:27-29).

Isn't this what we have seen historically? What did God do when He began to establish a race through which the Messiah should come? He started with Abraham, who came from a family of idol worshipers living in heathen Mesopotamia (Josh. 24:2-3, 14; Isa. 51:1-2). What did God do when he needed a Hebrew prime minister for Egypt? He took Joseph out of the king's prison (Gen. 41:14, 38-44). God called Moses when he was a sheep herder on the backside of the desert in Midian (Ex. 3:1-2). He called the disciples when they were fishermen and tax collectors (Mark 1:16-20; Matt. 9:9). He called Paul when he was vigorously persecuting Christ's followers (Acts 9).

God does the unexpected. And this means that God will often find His followers in lowly places. The Bible says, "For ye see your calling, brethren, how that not many wise men after the flesh, not many mighty, not many noble, are called; but God hath chosen the foolish things of the world to confound the wise; and God hath chosen the weak things of the world to confound the things which are mighty; and base things of the world, and things which are despised, hath God chosen, yea, and things which are not, to bring to nothing things that are, that no flesh should glory in His presence" (1 Cor. 1:26-29).

We see the truth of this principle in the sequel to God's calling of David.

Kings in Conflict

During my college years, I had the opportunity of studying under some great men, one of whom taught the basic course on Shakespeare at Harvard University. This man had many techniques by which he tried to engrave the plots of Shakespeare's plays on our minds. I remember that in teaching *Richard II,* he put a diagram on the blackboard to show how the plot hinges on the decline of Richard II, king of England at the beginning of the play, and the emergence of Bolingbroke, who becomes Henry IV toward the end.

The diagram was a large letter X, but instead of being upright it was lying on its side. The line that began at the top on the left represented Richard II. He starts out as king. But he makes tragic mistakes, is confined to prison, and eventually is killed. His line ends up on the bottom. The other line that began at the bottom on the left ends up on the top. It represents Bolingbroke, who starts from humble circumstances but passes Richard at about Act III and ends up as King Henry after Richard's execution.

This is precisely the plot that we have in the central part of the combined Books of 1 and 2 Samuel. King Saul declined from the throne of Israel to an ignominious death at the hands of the Philistines; David rose from the humblest of circumstances to arrive eventually at the throne. We may study this story, as others would study *Richard II,* trying to discern the reasons why Saul's course went downward while David succeeded. When we have found the reasons, we may apply them to ourselves personally.

Decline of King Saul

Why did Saul's reign spiral downward? First, we need to look at the course of his life. Saul seems to have begun quite acceptably. He was attractive and brave. But we are not far into the story (1 Sam. 13) when we find him making a tragic mistake. Saul had been commanded to remain at Gilgal until Samuel should come to him, but Samuel delayed. When Saul saw the distress of the people, he intruded into the office of the priests by performing a sacrifice in direct violation of the levitical Law.

No doubt Saul's motives were noble—he wanted help from the Lord; the people were frightened; the Philistines were on the verge of attacking. But the action was still wrong. The end did not justify the means. Thus when Samuel came, he rebuked Saul, warning him that his kingdom would not continue and that God had sought out another man to be king who would obey His commandments.

That was only the beginning. In chapter 14 of 1 Samuel, we find Saul making a foolish vow that nearly cost the life of his son Jonathan. In chapter 15, Saul is commanded to destroy the Amalekites completely, but we are told that he disobeyed, sparing "Agag, and the best of the sheep, and of the oxen, and of the fatlings, and the lambs, and all that was good" (v. 9). In chapter 18, Saul is consumed with jealousy of David. In chapters 19–27, he is pursuing David. In chapter 28, he consults the witch of Endor. In chapter 31, he dies.

Why did all this happen to Saul? The key is found in the story of Saul's incomplete obedience in regard to the destruction of the Amalekites. Here the prophet Samuel declares, "For rebellion is as the sin of witchcraft, and stubbornness is as iniquity and idolatry. Because thou hast rejected the word of the Lord, He hath also rejected thee from being king" (1 Sam. 15:23). The course of Saul's life from that point led downward because God had rejected him as king and had ceased to bless him. And why did God reject Saul? Because Saul had rejected God's word and consequently would not obey Him.

It is a tragic picture. It is doubly tragic in that it portrays the lives of so many in the Church of Jesus Christ today. Thousands of Christians today are more wrapped up in what the world has to say about expediency in business, laxity in morals, permissiveness with children, materialism, sex, prejudice, and other things than they are in the clear-cut Word of God. Whose word are you going to take? The word of the world? Or the Word of the living God?

The Upward Line

As the life of King Saul spiraled downward, the life of David moved upward. In David we find the secret of a life of great blessing.

We need to recognize, however, that at the beginning of David's public life the upward course was only internal; that is, it existed only in the development of the *character* of David. If we were to look only at outward circumstances, we would be tempted to say that David was declining while Saul was ascending.

What do we find? When David first comes to prominence, he is seen in the palace of the king; he is a great favorite because of his killing of Goliath (1 Sam. 18:2). A little later, he is out with the armies (1 Sam. 18:5). Later, his command is reduced (1 Sam. 18:13). Finally, after he has been obliged to run away from Saul, we find him in the cave of Adullam with only a handful of followers (1 Sam. 22:1-2).

Externally David's course was downward. But internally— that was something else! For all during this period, David grew spiritually. His faith grew. His understanding grew. He grew in his ability to govern men. God was using these difficult circumstances to prepare David for ruling Israel.

We must remember, too, that these were the days in which God was building David's army. In 1 Samuel 22:1-2 we read,

THE CHOICE OF A KING

"David, therefore, departed from there, and escaped to the cave, Adullam; and when his brethren and all his father's house heard it, they went down there to him. And every one who was in distress, and every one who was in debt, and every one who was discontented, gathered themselves unto him; and he became a captain over them: and there were with him about 400 men." In time (as we read in 1 Chronicles 12) this original 400 grew to 340,000 fighting men.

Who were the men whom God sent to David during this period of his banishment in the wilderness? Were they the well-trained troops of the king? Not at all. They were the little people of the land, those who were in distress, in debt, and discontented. Saul would no doubt have called these the off-scouring of the kingdom. But God had chosen to build the army of His king with these people.

This is a great spiritual lesson. For just as God chose the little people of David's time to do His work, so does He choose little people today. And He does it so that He, and not man, might have the glory.

Do you know that lesson? If you are trusting in your own wisdom and strength, as Saul did, God cannot use you. But if you will acknowledge your foolishness and weakness before Him, as David was forced to do, He will exalt Himself in you and lead you even in the most difficult circumstances.

Moreover, He will give you patience when events do not move quickly. We have traced the flight of David from the palace of King Saul to the cave of Adullam. There were yet more years of flight. There were years spent in Ziklag in Philistine territory, where David should not have been (1 Sam. 27–28). After the death of Saul, David reigned for seven and a half years in Hebron before he was welcomed as king over all Israel (2 Sam. 2:11). In all, there was a wait of perhaps 15 years. But David learned that if he was to be honored as king it would have to be God Himself who honored him. So he waited patiently. God can teach you this great lesson also.

David's Secret

In this study we have only briefly traced the years of David's exile and eventual rise. And we are still left with the question: What was the secret of David's success? Why did David's star rise higher and higher while Saul's star declined? The answer is simple. David kept his eyes on the Lord. Saul looked to his own wisdom and disobeyed, while David looked to the Lord and obeyed. We know, because David wrote a psalm about his experiences during the years when he hid from Saul in the cave—Psalm 57—and the whole psalm tells how David kept his eyes on the Lord even in the midst of adversities.

That was David's secret. You say, "Can that be my experience? Can God guide me through adversity?"

Yes, He can. In fact, He asks you to let Him provide such guidance. He says that if we keep our eyes on Him, He will bless and guide us. He says, "I will instruct thee and teach thee in the way which thou shalt go; I will guide thee with Mine eye" (Ps. 32:8).

WHEN GOD SAYS NO

(2 SAMUEL 7)

A familiar story tells of a little boy who was overheard praying for a bicycle for Christmas. When Christmas arrived and there was no bicycle, the person who had overheard the little boy's prayer asked him why God had not answered it. The little boy thought for a moment and then replied, "But He did answer it. He said No!"

That characterizes much of our own experience in prayer. There can be little doubt that no is an answer as well as yes. But if we think about it, most of us will agree that when we receive a yes to our prayer we consider the prayer answered, and when we receive a no we consider it unanswered. It seems that the second situation occurs as often as the first. Thus the problem of unanswered prayer—or of receiving a no—is a great one. One of the Bible's greatest characters asked God for something and received no for an answer. The meat of the story lies in the fact that he was praying, so far as we can tell, with the highest of spiritual motives. That person was King David, and his prayer was that he be allowed to build a great temple for the worship of God in Jerusalem.

The Bible tells us of David's plan and of the initial agreement of the Prophet Nathan to it in 2 Samuel 7:1-3: "And it came to pass, when the king sat in his house, and the Lord had given him rest round about from all his enemies, that the king said unto Nathan, the prophet, See, now, I dwell in an house of cedar, but the Ark of God dwelleth within curtains. And Nathan said to the king, Go, do all that is in thine heart; for the Lord is with thee."

Unanswered Prayer

We must begin with some consideration of what prayer is; for many persons do not understand the most basic facts about prayer and hence, do not have their prayers answered for quite obvious reasons. (If you are in this category, you must not think that the things said later in this study about David apply to your situation.)

There is much more in the Bible about God's *not* answering prayer than about His answering it. First, God will not ordinarily answer the prayer of a non-Christian. He offers salvation, and that is as broad as humanity. Anyone can come to God through faith in the Lord Jesus Christ. But there is not one promise of comfort, not one promise of provision, not one promise of help in times of distress or danger for anyone who is not a believer in the Lord Jesus Christ.

Someone will say, "But don't we read in the Bible, 'Ask, and it shall be given you; seek, and ye shall find; knock, and it shall be opened unto you'? And doesn't that mean that anyone can pray and receive an answer?"

No, that promise was not made to unbelievers—it was made to believers. The "you" of the verse—ask and it shall be given *you*; seek and *you* shall find; knock, and it shall be opened unto *you*—refers only to the believer. Even the well-known Lord's Prayer begins with this teaching, for it can only be prayed by those who can address God as their heavenly Father.

Second, the Bible says that God will not even hear the prayers of some Christians. For instance, He will not hear the prayer of one who is cherishing sin in his heart. This means that if you are living in sin with some person, or cheating some person, or harboring a grudge, you will find that God is ignoring the prayers for peace of mind, prosperity, and abundant life which you make on Sunday mornings or in your quiet time.

Isaiah knew this when he wrote, "Behold, the Lord's hand is not shortened, that it cannot save; neither His ear heavy, that it cannot hear. But your iniquities have separated between you and your God, and your sins have hidden His face from you, that He will not hear" (Isa. 59:1-2). Psalm 66:18 says, "If I regard iniquity in my heart, the Lord will not hear me."

The Bible also says that God will not answer a Christian's prayers if the Christian is praying out of His will. This is not surprising. For if God's will for us is the best thing that could possibly happen to us—which it is—then anything other than that would be harmful. God will not give us that which will harm us spiritually any more than a mother will give a shiny paring knife to a baby just because he cries for it. James is talking about this problem from the negative side when he writes, "Ye ask, and receive not, because ye ask amiss" (James 4:3). And John wrote positively, "And whatever we ask, we receive of Him, because we keep His commandments, and do those things that are pleasing in His sight" (1 John 3:22).

It is safe to say that billions of prayers are not answered simply because the persons praying are not Christians, and that millions more are not answered because—although they are prayed by Christians—the Christians are harboring some known sin or are praying foolishly. Many of our own prayers probably fall in at least one of these categories.

David's Prayer

These things that we have been discussing may apply to us, but they do not really apply to this period in the life of King David. We have been talking about prayers that are wrong or that are prayed by a person who is persisting in sin. But David prayed about building the Temple out of what appeared to be the purest and most noble of motives, at a time when he was in a right relationship with God.

First, he prayed *responsibly*. This is the real meaning of the first of the three verses quoted earlier, for we are told that the prayer was made after the Lord had given David "rest round about from all his enemies." If David had prayed this prayer during the period in his life when he was out fighting the Lord's battles, when he was overcoming the Philistines, Moabites, and Syrians, then the prayer would not have been responsible. God could rightly have said, "Forget that foolishness now. Your job is to win the next battle." However, that was not the time in which David prayed; he prayed in a time of peace and prosperity.

Do we pray responsibly? Some years ago a friend of mine, who lived in Los Angeles and who often preached there on weekends while he was going through school, told me a story that illustrates what many of us frequently do. He said that quite early one Sunday morning he set out with a friend to climb Mount Wilson, which is very close to Los Angeles. He had planned the climb to arrive at the top at 11 o'clock. He intended at that hour to ask God for a special sense of His presence and a new revelation of His will.

As he told me this I asked, "And did God answer your prayer?"

He replied, "God told me, 'You're supposed to be preaching at this very minute at a church in Los Angeles.'"

He had forgotten about it.

No doubt many of us find ourselves in such situations. But David was praying about the Temple only after his previous God-given responsibilities had been fulfilled.

Second, David prayed *unselfishly*. He might have argued that he needed a new wing on the palace or a new contingent of troops. Instead, he told Nathan, "See, now, I dwell in an house of cedar, but the ark of God dwelleth within curtains" (2 Sam. 7:2).

David also prayed *spiritually*. That is, he prayed with the express intention of pleasing God and doing His will.

Why do I say this? Because of two verses in the 12th chapter of Deuteronomy, which I believe David knew, and which may very well have given him the idea to build the temple in Jerusalem in the first place. These verses are part of God's instructions to Moses before the taking of the promised land. "But when ye go over the Jordan, and dwell in the land which the Lord your God giveth you to inherit, and when He giveth you rest from all your enemies around about, so that ye dwell in safety, then there shall be a place which the Lord your God shall choose to cause His name to dwell there" (Deut. 12:10-11).

If David knew these words, he would have viewed the events of his own lifetime as the fulfillment of the first part. And he would have thought that he was fulfilling the second part in obedience to the Lord when he planned to construct a temple where the true God would be worshiped.

Why God Says No

When we put all these truths together, we find that it is possible for a believer to be in a state in which he is not harboring known sin and to pray responsibly, unselfishly, and spiritually for a thing that is apparently God's will and yet have God say no.

Why does God say no? There are answers to this question that we will never know, at least not until we get to heaven. And yet there are answers that we can see and assimilate now. Many of these are seen in this story from 2 Samuel.

Why did God say no to David? What benefits resulted from that no? First, by means of this answer, David learned that he was not as necessary to God as he might have been tempted to think. In fact, he should have learned that he was not essential at all. This is the most significant point in the Lord's reply to David. God reminds David not of what David had done for Jehovah but of what Jehovah had done for David. Thus, God tells him, "I took thee from the sheepcote, from following the sheep, to be ruler over My people, over Israel; and I was with thee wherever thou wentest, and have cut off all thine enemies out of thy sight, and have made thee a great name, like unto the name of the great men who are in the earth" (2 Sam. 7:8-9).

This is something that we can all apply personally. Most of us believe, at least intellectually, that God can do whatever He wants to do without us. But somehow, when we are in the midst of His work, it is very easy to associate ourselves with the success of what God is doing. And we begin to wonder how the Lord could possibly manage without us. If you think this way, perhaps God has been saying no to your prayers in order that you might learn this lesson. Jesus said, "Without Me ye can do nothing" (John 15:5).

The second benefit of God's no was that David learned that God had a reason for what He was doing even though David was unable to see it at the time. David did learn the reason later. For when David spoke to Solomon about building the temple years later he said, "But the word of the Lord came to me, saying, Thou hast shed blood abundantly, and hast made great wars; thou shalt not build an house unto My name, because thou hast shed much blood upon the earth in My sight" (1 Chron. 22:8). Nevertheless, at this time David did not have the reason. Instead, he had to learn to trust God for it.

Do you do that? The patterns of God are often hard to detect in this life. Have you ever looked at a beautiful piece of tapestry from the wrong side? If you have, you know that the wrong side is a tangle of threads. At times a bit of the pattern can be traced, but it is largely unintelligible and confusing. Yet, when you turn the tapestry over, the pattern is beautiful and clearly apparent. In a similar way, life for us is often a tangle; we see it only from the wrong side. However, we are told that the day is coming when we shall see it from the right side—from God's perspective—and that in the meantime we are to trust Him to work out the pattern.

The third benefit from God's no to David was that He was free to say yes to David about something else. He said no so that he might be able to give David a better and different blessing that was uniquely his own.

What was the blessing? Well, David had told the Lord that he wanted to build Him a house. Instead, God promised David that He will build David a house. "Also the Lord telleth thee that He will make thee an house. And when thy days be fulfilled, and thou shalt sleep with thy fathers, I will set up thy seed after thee, which shall proceed out of thine own body, and I will establish His kingdom. . . . And thine house and thy kingdom shall be established forever before thee; thy throne shall be established forever" (2 Sam. 7:11-12, 16).

In other words, God was saying, "I don't want you to get wrapped up in building a temple. Instead, I am going to build you a house. That's better. And I am going to make it so permanent that when My Messiah comes We are going to speak of the permanence of His reign by reference to you. We will say that He will reign upon the throne of His father David forever."

God's Promises

David learned one more thing as he was faced with God's denial. David had prayed. God had said no. God gave a promise. Then—and this is the point—David learned to claim the promises of God for himself personally. Thus, in the midst of his second and much longer prayer, which closes this chapter (2 Sam. 7:18-29), David first confesses his own unworthiness and then prays, "And now, O Lord God, the word that Thou hast spoken concerning Thy servant, and concerning his house, establish it forever, and do as Thou hast said. And let Thy name be magnified forever, saying, The Lord of hosts is the God over Israel; and let the house of Thy servant, David, be established before Thee" (vv. 25-26).

If God says no to one of your prayers, it is not that you might become discouraged or confused. It is that you might be led to turn to His promises. What are your needs? Is your need for pardon of sins and forgiveness? The Bible says, "If we confess our sins, He is faithful and just to forgive us our sins, and to cleanse us from all unrighteousness" (1 John 1:9).

Is your need for peace? The Bible says, "Come unto Me, all ye that labor and are heavy laden, and I will give you rest" (Matt. 11:28). We read, "Thou wilt keep him in perfect peace, whose mind is stayed on Thee, because he trusteth in Thee (Isa. 26:3).

Is it for wisdom? "If any of you lack wisdom, let him ask of God, who giveth to all men liberally, and upbraideth not, and it shall be given him" (James 1:5).

Assurance? "My sheep hear My voice, and I know them, and they follow Me. And I give unto them eternal life; and they shall never perish, neither shall any man pluck them out of My hand" (John 10:27-28).

And, just in case some need has been left out, we also read, "But my God shall supply all your need according to His riches in glory by Christ Jesus" (Phil. 4:19).

There is no need in your life, however great or small, that is not covered somewhere in the Word of God by such promises. And the promises are there in order that we might learn to claim them. If God says no to one of your prayers (and the reason is not one of the things that we considered earlier in this study), He only wishes to bring you greater blessing. Trust Him. Learn to claim His promises of blessing personally.

WHEN BELIEVERS SIN

(2 SAMUEL 11–19)

Some time ago, in a question-and-answer period, someone asked, "Doctor Boice, is it possible for a Christian to commit murder?"

I suppose the questioner held the view that there should always be a basic minimum of sanctification in a Christian that prohibits such things. But I answered as I always answer such questions, saying, "Yes, a Christian can certainly do that."

A Christian can murder, steal, commit adultery, run off and leave his family, and allow his life to be filled with such bitterness that he is a terror to all around him. In general, a Christian can make a total wreck of his life. The Bible itself suggests this when it warns Christians against such sins.

We must not think, of course, that God will permit sin in the life of a Christian to go undisciplined. And we must acknowledge that there is generally a point in our lives beyond which He will not let us go. We all sin, in big ways or little ways. We taste its consequences. Sin turns ugly. Pleasures turn to dust in our mouths. But this happens so that we will come to the point—as God intends—when we will yearn for the joy we once knew, and will turn to Him for His perfect forgiveness and cleansing.

We come now to an incident in the life of King David in which this greatest of all Israel's kings, the one who was called "a man after God's own heart," sinned by committing adultery and then compounded that sin by an act of murder. It is a sad and solemn record. But we turn to it humbly in order that we might learn something of the depth of our own human depravity and that we might learn how to turn to God for cleansing.

The Sin of King David

The Bible says that in the time of the year when kings went forth to battle, that is, in the spring after the enforced inactivity of winter, David sent Joab and the troops of Israel out against the Ammonites. "But David," we are told, "tarried still at Jerusalem" (2 Sam. 11:1). It is an ominous "but" for it indicates the disapproval by the Lord of David's action. During this period, David saw Bathsheba bathing on a roof nearby. He sent messengers to find out who she was. They brought back word: "Is not this Bathsheba, the daughter of Eliam, the wife of Uriah, the Hittite?" (v. 3)

That should have been the end of the matter for David; Bathsheba was another man's wife. But instead, he took her to himself and later learned that she had conceived a child by him. We can imagine that at this point David's blood ran hot and cold. But instead of confessing his sin, he set out upon a course that greatly compounded it.

First, he invited Uriah home from the battle on the pretext of learning about it, hoping that the man would spend a few nights at home with his wife so that he could be identified as the father of the child. However, Uriah was more conscious of his duty than King David was of his. He would not go home but said, "The Ark, and Israel, and Judah abide in tents; and my lord, Joab, and the servants of my lord, are encamped in the open fields. Shall I, then, go into mine house, to eat and to drink, and to lie with my wife? As thou livest, and as thy soul liveth, I will not do this thing" (v. 11).

Uriah refused to go home, even when David made him drunk. Therefore, David sent a note to Joab by the hand of Uriah saying that Uriah was to be placed in a position in the battle where the fighting was hottest, abandoned, and left to be killed.

Joab must have wondered how David, the man who could write such beautiful, spiritual poetry and who would not act against King Saul, could command such a murder. For murder it was. Nevertheless, he did as David commanded. Uriah died. David breathed a sigh of relief and satisfaction. Yet we read: "But the thing that David had done displeased the Lord" (v. 27).

Repentance

Matthew Henry, the well-known Bible expositor, once said, "Though God may suffer His people to fall into sin, He will not suffer His people to lie still in it." This is quite true. Thus, instead of abandoning David, God sent the Prophet Nathan to confront him with his sin. Because of this David repented.

Nathan had said, "Thou art the man" (2 Sam. 12:7).

And David replied, "I have sinned against the Lord" (v. 13).

On the basis of that confession, God forgave David's sin— although he still had to suffer many of the consequences of it—and restored him to complete fellowship.

But how can a righteous God restore to fellowship a man

who has committed adultery and then murdered an innocent man? The important answer to that question lies in a great psalm that David wrote as the result of this incident in his life. For if we understand this psalm, we can understand not only how God could forgive King David but also how God can forgive us, no matter how great or small our sins may be.

Psalm 51 begins, "Have mercy upon me, O God, according to Thy loving-kindness; according unto the multitude of Thy tender mercies blot out my transgressions" (v. 1). Notice how many times this single verse speaks of God's mercies: "Have *mercy* upon me . . . according to Thy *loving-kindness;* according to the multitude of Thy tender *mercies.*" Three times! Thus, when David turned again to God in the aftermath of his sin, the first thing he asserts is his confidence in God's mercy.

Now and then, as I speak to people who do not know the Lord, someone will say that he only wants justice from God. And I say, woe to that person. The man who wants only justice from God will receive hell and spiritual death, for death is the just punishment for sin (Rom. 6:23). How wonderful to know that instead of coming to God on the basis of His justice, we can come on the basis of His mercy, the way David came.

Confession of Sin

The *basis* of forgiveness for sin, then, lies in God's mercy. But this is only the first of several principles that we must apply in our search for forgiveness.

The second is that the *condition* for forgiveness of sin lies in our confession of it. As soon as David recalled God's mercy, he immediately confessed his sin: "For I acknowledge my transgressions, and my sin is ever before me. Against Thee, Thee only, have I sinned, and done this evil in Thy sight, that Thou mightest be justified when Thou speakest, and be clear when Thou judgest" (Ps. 51:3-4).

David laid his sin before the Lord and confessed it utterly. This is the significance of verse four: "Against Thee, Thee only, have I sinned." Many people have observed that this was not entirely true. David had sinned against Bathsheba, as well as with her. He had sinned against Uriah, her husband. He had sinned against the armies of Israel, who lost a battle during the time of David's sin. He had sinned against the nation. Above all, however, he had sinned against God. And in his own mind this greatly overshadowed the other aspects of his offense.

How great a difference there would be in your life and mine if we would only see our sin for what it is in God's sight and confess it openly.

Cleansing

The first step in David's great prayer is the *basis* of forgiveness—God's mercy. The second step is the *condition* of forgiveness—the confession of the sin itself. The third step is the *means* of receiving forgiveness—atonement and renewal. David says, "Purge me with hyssop, and I shall be clean; wash me, and I shall be whiter than snow" (v. 7).

Why does David say, "Purge me with hyssop"? Hyssop was a little plant that grew throughout the ancient Near East and was used in the sacrifices of temple worship. The plant, which was only 6'-10" high, was broken off at the stem and bound to a short stick with a scarlet cord. This made a small brush. It was then used to sprinkle the blood of the sacrifice either upon the doorposts of the house (as had been done on the evening of the Passover in Egypt) or upon the worshipers. Consequently, hyssop spoke of sacrifices and of the atonement provided for sin. David is saying, "I come confident of

Thy mercy, acknowledging my sin; but I also acknowledge that I need to have an atonement for my sin."

Finally, David says that he needs renewal. "Create in me a clean heart, O God, and renew a right spirit within me" (v. 10). These words acknowledged that in addition to the cleansing that was his by means of the sacrifice, David also needed to receive a new inner nature. The word translated *create* in this verse is the word *bara*, the same word used in the first verses of Genesis to describe God's Creation of the world out of nothing. Thus when David says, "Create in me a clean heart," he means, "Bring a new nature into existence out of nothing."

The Bible teaches that there is no good in man that can satisfy God (Rom. 3:10-20). But it also teaches that God can and does plant a new nature within the person who comes to him (2 Cor. 5:17; Col. 3:9-10). Where there was nothing but sin before, there is now a new nature which alone is capable of pleasing Him.

The Consequences of Sin

We now move in our study to a very difficult subject—the consequences of sin. Does the believer experience some or all of the natural consequences of sin in his life even though he has been forgiven by God? The natural answer of our hearts is no. Of course not! If God forgives He forgives utterly, and so He removes the consequences also.

But the fact is that God does *not* cancel out all the consequences of sin. This truth is nowhere better illustrated than in the later incidents of David's life. The whole story of the rebellion of David's son Absalom (2 Sam. 13–19), is an example. The judgment which God pronounced on David and his family because of his sin with Bathsheba is recorded in 2 Samuel 12:10-12. "Now, therefore, the sword shall never depart from thine house, because thou hast despised Me, and hast taken the wife of Uriah, the Hittite, to be thy wife. Thus saith the Lord, Behold, I will raise up evil against thee out of thine own house, and I will take thy wives before thine eyes, and give them unto thy neighbor, and he shall lie with thy wives in the sight of this sun. For thou didst it secretly; but I will do this thing before all Israel, and before the sun.''

A study of the context of these verses reveals that immediately after this, David confessed and was assured by the Prophet Nathan that he had forgiveness. Nevertheless, the events that God had spoken of in His words of judgment fell exactly as He had said.

This challenges us because it is precisely opposite from the way we think of forgiveness. What do we mean when we say that we are ready to forgive someone? We usually mean, ''I'll forgive, but I'll never forget.'' We forgive to the extent of not insisting on retribution or on the prosecution of the law, but the fellowship that previously existed between ourselves and the other person is broken beyond recovery. We waive the law but break the fellowship. God in His perfect forgiveness does just the opposite. He restores the fellowship, but He does not eliminate all the natural consequences of our rebellion.

Human Forgiveness

Each of these two types of forgiveness—man's and God's—is illustrated by David's story. David had sinned against Bathsheba and against her husband Uriah, first by committing adultery with the wife and second by arranging to have the husband killed in battle. The time came, however, when the very things that David had practiced against Bathsheba and Uriah began to occur in his own household. It almost seemed as if a cord had snapped at the time of David's sin, with the result that immorality began to increase within the palace. First, Amnon, the oldest of David's sons, developed a passionate fixation for Tamar, the sister of Absalom, David's son by another wife. Amnon conceived a plan by which Tamar was brought to him privately, and then he raped her. Amnon did to Tamar what David had done to Bathsheba. We read that when David heard about it he "was very angry" (2 Sam. 13:21).

David was not the only one who heard of the crime, however. Absalom, Tamar's brother, also heard of his sister's mistreatment, and he began to plan for a way to repay Amnon. After two years had passed, Absalom sprang a trap in which Amnon was murdered. Then, in order to save his own life, Absalom fled. David remained in Jerusalem and mourned angrily for his son.

Imperfect Restoration

At this point, Joab reentered the picture with a scheme to restore Absalom to David's favor (2 Sam. 14). Joab appears to have been a shrewd and unprincipled politician. He had unscrupulously carried out the king's orders to have Uriah killed. Now he was equally unscrupulous in trying to get Absalom back into the palace. He probably said to himself, "Absalom is doubtless the one whom David would like to have become king since Amnon is dead, and he is best suited for it. He is handsome—a bit willful perhaps—but the one who can win the favor of the people. If I can restore good feelings between Absalom and David, I will both please David and endear myself to Absalom." So he plotted.

We read that Joab arranged for a woman to come to David with a sad story that concerned her two sons. One had killed the other and now, so she said, the whole family was demanding that the remaining son be punished. She asked for a merciful intervention, David, in disregard of the Law, responded, "As the Lord liveth, there shall not one hair of thy son fall to the earth" (2 Sam. 14:11).

The king was caught. The woman applied her story to the case of Absalom, and David reluctantly agreed to let Absalom come back. Only for over two years Absalom was not allowed to see his father face to face (2 Sam. 14:24, 28). From that point it was only a short step to Absalom's political rebellion (2 Sam. 15:1-12), David's flight from Jerusalem (2 Sam. 15:13–16:14), the literal fulfillment of God's judgments against David (2 Sam. 16:21-22), and the final battle in which Absalom was killed (2 Sam. 18).

David's forgiveness of Absalom, such as it was, illustrates our forgiveness. We waive the law, as David did, but we do not restore fellowship. We will forgive, but not forget. God forgets the sin as far as fellowship with Himself is concerned. Nevertheless, sin has certain temporal consequences.

A Few Conclusions

There are conclusions to be drawn from this study of the life of David, whatever your position before God. Perhaps you have never turned to the Lord Jesus Christ for salvation, thinking that God will "forgive" you in the way that we naturally think of forgiveness. You may be expecting God somehow to overlook the demands of His law and justice and to tolerate your willfulness and rebellion. But God does not work that way. God considers the punishment of sin so important and so necessary that He sent His own Son, Jesus Christ, to die for your sin in order to bear its punishment. Salvation consists of believing that Jesus Christ did that for you and committing your life to Him.

Perhaps you are a Christian but have become sloppy in your relationship to God. You argue wrongly that God will somehow take care of you and work everything out, even if you do as you please. You feel that you can dally with sin and get away with it. But God's love demands fatherly chastisement. If you persist in your own way, God will send judgment. At the very least your life will be unhappy and will lose its natural joy. At the worst, God will break your life into little pieces until you learn what kind of God you are dealing with and come to appreciate the One who has called you to be His own.

You may be one who is walking in God's way but has failed to practice true forgiveness with friends or family. Like David, you have broken the fellowship but waived the discipline. There is no surer way to produce problem children or weaken a friendship or a marriage. If you are in a position to exercise discipline, as with children, it is your duty to do it. But it must be done in love and without destroying the fellowship.

Perhaps you are saying that this cannot be done—that you cannot do it. That is right. In yourself you cannot, for this is divine love and divine forgiveness. And yet, the Lord Jesus Christ can exercise His love and forgiveness through you if you are a Christian and will allow Him to do it.

DAVID AND DAVID'S LORD

(2 SAMUEL 23:1-7)

Many years ago on a Christmas day, my great-grandfather died. He had been ailing for some time and had been confined to his bedroom. Because of Christmas, however, the family had brought him out to the living room where he was placed on a sofa. The morning passed, and the afternoon came. Grandfather began to speak with those members of the family who were present about the Lord Jesus Christ and His second coming. Suddenly, while he was speaking, he drew himself upward off the sofa, stretching out his hands toward heaven. A big smile crossed his face; his eyes lighted up. Then he fell back, having gone to be with his Lord. The family was convinced that he had caught a vision of Jesus at the moment of his homegoing.

I tell this story because it is somewhat analogous to an experience which David had shortly before his death, an experience which highlights David's life-long expectation of the Messiah. What David saw may or may not have been seen with the eyes; yet it was a true vision of the coming of the Lord Jesus Christ.

DAVID AND DAVID'S LORD

The incident is recorded in 2 Samuel 23:1-7. "Now these are the last words of David. David, the son of Jesse, said, . . . 'The Spirit of the Lord spoke by me, and His word was in my tongue.' The God of Israel said, 'the Rock of Israel spoke to me, He who ruleth over men must ʰe just, ruling in the fear of God. And He shall be as the light ot ᴄhe morning, when the sun riseth, even a morning without clouds, as the tender grass springing out of the earth by clear shining after rain. Although my house is not so with God, yet He hath made with me an everlasting covenant, ordered in all things, and sure; for this is all my salvation, and all my desire, although He maketh it not to grow. But the worthless men shall be all of them as thorns thrust away. . . . They shall be utterly burned with fire in the same place.' "

A Prophecy

If we are to understand this difficult passage of Scripture, we must begin by realizing that it is a prophecy. This is the significance of the first sentence: "Now these are the last words of David." If that phrase—*the last words*—is taken in a literal sense, it is contradicted by the fact that David actually speaks other things later, for example, in chapter 24 or in 1 Kings. But if it is taken as a statement that these are the last *inspired* words of David, then it makes sense. This is what is emphasized by the fourfold repetition of the truth that *God is speaking* through him. Thus we read, "The Spirit of the Lord spoke by me, and His word was in my tongue. The God of Israel said, the Rock of Israel spoke to me."

The second fact that we should recognize is that the prophecy is speaking of the coming of the Lord Jesus Christ. It is true that at first reading some of the phrases could be taken to mean that any king must be just or honest: "He who ruleth over men must be just, ruling in the fear of God." But this

133

interpretation does not hold up for the whole section, for in succeeding verses David is contrasting the failures of his household with God's ways of real justice and faithfulness. Hence it is on the basis of what God will do, rather than what man can do, that David speaks of the Just Ruler who shall be as the light of the morning and who shall fulfill the everlasting covenant. And He, the Lord, is David's salvation and David's desire.

Alexander Maclaren, a great expositor of the Bible, saw this clearly, and he has left us an excellent paragraph on David's final vision in *Expositions of Second Samuel and the Books of Kings*. He writes, "It was fitting that 'the last words of David' should be a prophecy of the true King, whom his own failures and sins, no less than his consecration and victories, had taught him to expect. His dying eyes see on the horizon of the far-off future the form of Him who is to be a just and perfect Ruler, before the brightness of whose presence and the refreshing of whose influence, verdure and beauty shall clothe the world. As the shades gather round the dying monarch, the radiant glory to come brightens. He departs in peace, having seen the salvation from afar, and stretched out longing hands of greeting toward it. Then his harp is silent, as if the rapture which thrilled the trembling strings had snapped them." *(Expositions of Holy Scripture*, Vol. II, Alexander Maclaren, Eerdmans, Grand Rapids, Mich.)

The Coming King

There are, of course, other texts from David's writings which have also been interpreted as messianic, and these are instructive too. For instance, consider the seventh chapter of 2 Samuel. That chapter contains God's promise to David of an everlasting kingdom and throne as well as David's response in prayer to that promise.

DAVID AND DAVID'S LORD

God had told David that He was going to establish David's throne forever and ever. But when David begins to answer, the first thing he acknowledges is that this is not after the manner of men, for whom everything eventually passes away. It is of God. Is God not really speaking of the Messiah, then? David asks.

The English text of 2 Samuel 7:19 says, "And is this the manner of man, O Lord God?" But this is not correct according to the Hebrew. The Hebrew text does not say "man" or "a man." It says "*the* man," who must therefore be the specific Son of man, the Messiah, whom David mentions elsewhere in the psalms. Apparently David recognized that only the Messiah would be able to establish his throne forever.

David's expectation of the Messiah is also evident in the first verse of Psalm 110, which we should consider with even greater care. Once when I was preaching on the psalms and had come to this verse, I began my message by asking the congregation what they thought was the Old Testament verse most quoted in the New Testament. I helped them out by suggesting Habakkuk 2:4, "The just shall live by his faith." That verse is quoted three time in the New Testament. I also suggested Genesis 15:6, which tells us that Abraham "believed in the Lord; and He counted it to him for righteousness." Paul refers to that verse several times. Yet it is neither of these.

The verse of the Old Testament that is most quoted in the New Testament is Psalm 110:1: "The Lord said unto my Lord, 'Sit Thou at My right hand, until I make Thine enemies Thy footstool.' " That verse is quoted at least 27 times, either in whole or in part. There is one reference each in the Books of Colossians, Ephesians, 1 Peter, 1 Corinthians, and Romans; three references in Luke; four in Matthew, Mark, and Acts; and six in the letter to the Hebrews.

Always the reference is concerned with bringing glory to Jesus Christ as the One whose coming was foretold in the Old Testament Scriptures.

It is easy to see why this saying of David's was so popular with the early Christians. In the first place, it refers to a plurality in the Godhead—"the Lord [Jehovah] said unto my Lord [the Messiah]"—and thus may be quoted in support of a claim to divinity on the part of Jesus Christ.

We must remember that when the first preachers of the Gospel went forth, they preached to Jews, and the Jewish people believed in the unity of God. "Hear, O Israel: The Lord our God is one Lord" (Deut. 6:4). This was a great obstacle to be overcome, for all Christian truth depended on the fact that Jesus Christ is God. Thus, the New Testament preachers must have searched the Old Testament for those verses which would speak of Christ's divinity. And they must have had some difficulty, because the doctrine is certainly not set forth in the Old Testament in the way in which it is set forth in the New Testament.

This does not mean that there are no intimations of Christ's divinity in the Old Testament, of course. We find one such intimation in the early chapters of Genesis. For there, at the beginning of the Hebrew Bible, the God who is over all is given a plural name—Elohim. This is not an accident as it would be in our day for someone who had the last name of *Persons*, or another name ending with an *s;* for the verses go right on to say, "Let *Us* make man in *Our* image." Thus, a plurality in the Godhead is indicated in the very first chapter of the Bible.

A plurality in the Godhead is also suggested in a number of other passages, but none is so obvious as Psalm 110:1. This verse clearly teaches the existence of God in more than one person, and it was therefore frequently referred to by the New Testament writers. In fact, Jesus Himself used the verse to prove to the rulers of His day that the Messiah, the coming One, must be divine (Matt. 22:44).

David's Lord

The significance of the verse rests upon the fact that it is David speaking in the psalm. Critical scholars of our day have recognized this and have attacked the verse by arguing that one of David's underlings was writing. Hence, they say, the psalm is a form of flattery. They suppose it to mean that Jehovah spoke to David saying, "Sit thou at My right hand, until I make thine enemies thy footstool."

This is not acceptable. For one thing, the psalm is clearly identified in the Hebrew Bible as a psalm of David. No one reading it before the growth of higher criticism in the 19th century would ever have taken it as being written about David by someone else. Moreover, the psalm speaks of the coming One as being a priest forever after the order of Melchizedek, and David was never a priest. He was not allowed to fulfill the functions of a priest, never made claims to being a priest, and never served as a priest.

Consequently, the verse must refer to someone other than David and, more than that, someone greater than David; for David acknowledges this One as his Lord. Clearly, the verse speaks of Jesus Christ, who at that time had not yet come, but who will yet sit on David's throne forever.

A Finished Work

There is another reason why this verse in Psalm 110 was so popular with the New Testament writers. It spoke not only of the divinity of Jesus; it spoke also of His finished work. How does the verse read? "The Lord said unto my Lord, *Sit* thou at My right hand." No one sits until he has finished the job which he has been given to do. Christ finished His work and, having finished it, took His rightful seat at the right hand of the Father.

The background for this lies in the nature of Jewish temple worship. The Jewish temple at Jerusalem was constructed in such a way that sacrifices could be performed daily for the sins of individuals and once a year in a special way for the sins of the nation.

Within the holiest part of the temple, the holy of holies, there was a gold-covered box surmounted by a replica of two cherubim with wings outstretched over the box (Ex. 25:10-22). It was called the ark of the covenant. Beneath the wings of the cherubim on the cover of the Ark was a place called the mercy seat where the blood was placed by the high priest on the Day of Atonement (Lev. 16:14-15). Within the ark were the Law of Moses and Aaron's rod that budded (Deut. 10:5; Num. 17:10).

Other things were also in the temple, including a seven-branch candlestick and the table for the showbread (Ex. 25:23-40). Outside the temple, in the courtyard, were an altar representing atonement (Ex. 27:1-8) and a laver used for purification (Ex. 30:17-21).

Among all these furnishings, however, there was not a single chair. The priests did not sit down. This was intentional. It was symbolic, for every aspect of the temple worship spoke of spiritual things. The absence of chairs symbolized that the work that was done by the priests throughout the hundreds of years of Jewish history was a work that was never completed. Sacrifices were offered in that temple courtyard every day, year after year, decade after decade, century after century. Millions upon millions of animals were slain. Once a year on the Day of Atonement the high priest carried the blood of the lamb into the holy of holies, placing it upon the mercy seat beneath the wings of the cherubim. This also went on year after year, decade after decade.

Yet all these sacrifices were brought to an end in Jesus Christ. Jesus was the great High Priest who offered Himself once for the sins of mankind and, having made the perfect sacrifice and having completed His work, sat down at the right hand of God. Thus, the author of Hebrews, who was writing primarily to Jewish people, observed, "And every priest standeth daily ministering and offering often the same sacrifices, which can never take away sins; but this Man, after He had offered one sacrifice for sins forever, sat down on the right hand of God, from henceforth expecting till His enemies be made His footstool. For by one offering He hath perfected forever them that are sanctified" (Heb. 10:11-14). That is our greatest assurance in the Christian life. Jesus Christ, having finished His work, sat down at God's right hand. When He said, "It is finished" (John 19:30), it was finished forever.

In the eighth chapter of Romans, the Apostle Paul also shows this event to be the Christian's security. He has just talked about the way our sins have been dealt with in Christ's death, and he turns to those who may still be uncertain about their security in Christ. He asks, "What shall we then say to these things? If God be for us, who can be against us? . . . Who shall lay any thing to the charge of God's elect? Shall God that justifieth? Who is he that condemneth? Shall Christ that died, yea rather, that is risen again, who is even at the right hand of God, who also maketh intercession for us?" (Rom. 8:31, 33-34). Charles Wesley knew this truth and wrote:

> Arise, my soul, arise, shake off thy guilty fears;
> The bleeding Sacrifice in my behalf appears:
> Before the Throne my Surety stands;
> My name is written on His hands.

He ever lives above, for me to intercede,
His all redeeming love, His precious blood to
  plead;
His blood atoned for every race,
And sprinkles now the Throne of grace.

Five bleeding wounds He bears, received on
  Calvary;
They pour effectual prayers, they strongly
  plead for me.
Forgive him, O forgive, they cry,
Nor let that ransomed sinner die.

The Father hears Him pray, His dear anointed
  One;
He cannot turn away the presence of His Son:
His Spirit answers to the blood,
And tells me I am born of God.

My God is reconciled; His pardoning voice I
  hear;
He owns me for His child, I can no longer fear;
With confidence I now draw nigh,
And "Father, Abba, Father!" cry.

So let no one disturb you with thoughts of an insecure
salvation. The salvation of a Christian rests upon the finished
work of Christ. It does not rest upon what we have done, nor
what we will do, but upon what Christ did once on the cross
of Calvary. In order that we might never doubt it, He is
seated at the right hand of God the Father Almighty,
having completed the work that His Father gave Him to
do.

DAVID AND DAVID'S LORD

A Final Victory

In terms of our salvation the work is done, but there is another work that is yet to be done. What does the verse say? "Sit Thou at my right hand, *until* I make Thine enemies Thy footstool." The day is coming when Jesus will rule over all things, but as yet we do not see all things put under Him.

There are those, even in the Christian Church, who have taught that the world is gradually getting better and better day by day. Christians who hold this position generally assert that they are helping to make it so and that the time will eventually come when all will be brought into God's fold. This is a form of universalism. But it is not the teaching of Scripture. The Bible teaches that there will always be enemies of Jesus Christ, and that God withholds His final judgment only until He can gather to Himself those whom He will call. The thousands of years of human history are to be understood, therefore, not as an ongoing march of progress or victory brought about by the effort of man, but as that period of time during which God calls unto Himself a holy people.

All paths do not comprise one road leading us all to the same end, a road that needs to be better and better paved as we advance to the goal. No, there is a broad road that leads to destruction. And now and then along that road, God turns somebody off onto the straight path that leads to life. Our verse teaches that this process will go on throughout history until the day that God calls it all to a halt and by force subdues Christ's enemies. They will be His enemies as much at the end as they were at the beginning, but they will be subdued, for we are told that before Christ every knee shall bow and every tongue shall confess that Christ is Lord to the glory of God the Father.

Portraits of Christ

As we have studied the life of King David, we have seen a bit of the glory of the Lord Jesus Christ portrayed in David's life and in the lessons which God taught him. I have been told that somewhere in Russia there is a palace containing a famous "Hall of Beauty." In this room are hung more than 850 portraits of young women painted by Count Rotari for the Empress Catherine the Second. The artist journeyed through all the 50 provinces of Russia to find his models. It is said, however, that when he had finished, the 850 portraits bore an unusual resemblance to Catherine the Second, by whom they were commissioned. For, in each picture, either by some gesture, pose, facial characteristic, jewel, flower, dress, or occupation, there was a delicate reference to the empress.

The story is an example of the way we attempt to flatter other human beings. But it is also an apt illustration of one way in which God has revealed Jesus Christ to us in His Word. Those who have been called by God, whose stories have been told in the Scriptures—men like Abraham, Moses, and David—are in one sense God's pictures. They are painted by Him through His grace, and in them some of the characteristics of Jesus Christ may be seen. We ought now to turn from the portraits to the One who is Himself altogether lovely and for whom and by whom they were commissioned.